Reputation Management

Gerry Griffin

MARKETING

04.05

■ Fast track route to mastering all aspects of reputation management

■ Covers all the key techniques for successful reputation management, from understanding interest groups to communicating key messages, and from selecting the best channels to developing a tactical plan

■ Examples and lessons from some of the world's most successful businesses, including Unilever, Bitor and Royal Dutch Shell

■ Includes a glossary of key concepts and a comprehensive resources guide

>>EXPRESS EXEC. COM<<
essential management thinking at your fingertips

Copyright © Capstone Publishing 2002

The right of Gerry Griffin to be identified as the author of this work has been asserted in accordance with the Copyright, Designs and Patents Act 1988

First published 2002 by
Capstone Publishing (a Wiley company)
8 Newtec Place
Magdalen Road
Oxford OX4 1RE
United Kingdom
http://www.capstoneideas.com

CIP catalogue records for this book are available from the British Library and the US Library of Congress

ISBN 1-84112-231-9

Printed and bound in Great Britain

This book is printed on acid-free paper

Substantial discounts on bulk quantities of Capstone books are available to corporations, professional associations and other organizations. Please contact Capstone for more details on +44 (0)1865 798 623 or (fax) +44 (0)1865 240 941 or (e-mail) info@wiley-capstone.co.uk

Contents

Introduction to ExpressExec

ExpressExec is 3 million words of the latest management thinking compiled into 10 modules. Each module contains 10 individual titles forming a comprehensive resource of current business practice written by leading practitioners in their field. From brand management to balanced scorecard, ExpressExec enables you to grasp the key concepts behind each subject and implement the theory immediately. Each of the 100 titles is available in print and electronic formats.

Through the ExpressExec.com Website you will discover that you can access the complete resource in a number of ways:

» printed books or e-books;
» e-content – PDF or XML (for licensed syndication) adding value to an intranet or Internet site;
» a corporate e-learning/knowledge management solution providing a cost-effective platform for developing skills and sharing knowledge within an organization;
» bespoke delivery – tailored solutions to solve your need.

Why not visit www.expressexec.com and register for free key management briefings, a monthly newsletter and interactive skills checklists. Share your ideas about ExpressExec and your thoughts about business today.

Please contact elound@wiley-capstone.co.uk for more information.

Introduction to Reputation Management

» Corporate communication is increasingly important for business success.
» Corporate communication can look to and shape the future.
» The starting point for corporate communication is the area that needs most attention: setting out the objectives of the business.
» Managers often fail to communicate the business objectives and are poor examples of communication in action.

August Busch III, head of Anheuser-Busch, the world's largest brewer, once ended his section of an annual report with a single exhortation: "Sell more beer." Interestingly, this command related to the company's commitment to protecting natural habitats, aluminum recycling, and other activities, voiced elsewhere in the report. Busch was creating the virtuous circle of enlightened self-interest. Help others but never forget that if we do not drive our business (which is selling beer) we won't be around to help anyone.

It raises an important issue: how do the activities of a company and the ways in which they are presented influence sales activity? Was Busch stating the unvarnished truth or was his message and how it was communicated actually likely to damage sales?

How senior managers communicate corporate messages is of increasing importance. Indeed, everything they say is a corporate message, dissected and analyzed by a range of audiences. What they communicate has a direct effect on the bottom line. Consider how the Body Shop's stance on animal testing and fair trading has helped to differentiate its products from those of other cosmetic retailers. Anita Roddick, the company's founder, is unlikely to call for Body Shop employees to "sell more moisturizer." Indeed, she says: "I can't take moisture cream too seriously – what interests me is the revolutionary way trade can be used as an instrument for change."[1]

Corporate communication can look to and shape the future. It can take up indirect or long-term topics to create or maintain sales; for example, by lobbying regulatory authorities to permit the use of genetically modified foodstuffs.

Some dismiss corporate communication as mere tactical maneuvering. Some argue that a company needs to be more than just the sum of its sales and marketing parts; that a company must offer more than just employment, tax revenue, and, of course, its goods or services.

Academic Sumantra Ghoshal has argued that corporations create social value. To see them merely as vehicles for shareholder value is blinkered: "Amid a general decline in the authority of other institutions – political parties, churches, the community, even the family unit – corporations have emerged as the most influential institutions of modern society; not only in creating and distributing a large part of its wealth, but also providing a social context for most of its people, thereby acting as a source of individual satisfaction and social succour."[2]

Thus, if a company is to communicate effectively, it must have a clear sense of what it is as an entity. In this sense, corporate communications should be applied common sense.

The starting point for corporate communications is the area that needs most attention: setting out the objectives of the business. A snapshot of most activity would contain some or all of the following:

» donorship to charities or artistic foundations;
» corporate advertising;
» initiatives with non-governmental organizations, such as Friends of the Earth;
» meetings with analysts; and
» local community initiatives.

If a company is unsure how its business interests are being served by any of these activities, then both the activity and any communications surrounding it are likely to lack rigor. In poorly communicating companies, explanations range from the traditional ("we're doing it because we've always done it") to patronage ("the chairman thinks it's a good idea") and philanthropy ("it's a good cause").

It may well be a good cause. But there are many good causes and selection must be based on rigorous criteria. Formulating a clear objective takes good leadership; to implement and assess it takes good management.

Often managers both fail to communicate the business objectives and are poor examples of communication in action. Management consultancy SKAI believes that when leaders communicate badly it is because they:

» abdicate responsibility to the corporate communications department;
» blandly give out the "corporate" message, giving nothing of themselves in either content or delivery;
» talk at too high a level, which rarely works internally;

» sanitize their words; and
» don't have a decision-making process on making information available, and therefore never get information out in a timely manner.

At a company-wide level, corporate communications require staff to have a clear picture of what they are trying to achieve as a business. A consistent message should be delivered through credible channels and timed for maximum impact. The company must:

» acknowledge business objectives;
» define the type of organization (what is the corporate culture?); and
» decide what it expects to gain from communicating either its corporate values or its corporate activities.

This work will examine the management of reputation at a corporate level – as distinct from brand or product reputation management. In this way, it will look at how you as an overall organization communicate to a range of key audiences in order to enhance the achievement of your business objectives.

ROADMAP

To start with, we will define what reputation is and how it works at a corporate level. Essential to the good practice of reputation management is a keen understanding of which audiences (e.g. government or non-governmental organizations) are important for your business health. These audiences will be detailed in full.

We will then take a brief look at the history of reputation management. It is a relatively new discipline, particularly when used for corporate ends, but public relations, media relations, and government lobbying all found expression in the last century. Two major recent (and related) trends which are set to grow in influence in this new millennium are the digital age and globalization. We will examine both of these key trends in detail before going on to look at what public and social obligations the modern day corporation is supposed to meet. This can be termed corporate social responsibility, which is a key aspect of corporate reputation management. Finally, we will go through how you might devise and implement a reputation management plan.

NOTES

1 Quoted in (1999) *Transnational Management: Text, Cases, and Readings in Cross Border Management.* McGraw-Hill Higher Education, New York.
2 Ghoshal, S. (1999) *The Individualized Corporation: A Fundamentally New Approach to Management*. HarperCollins Business, New York.

Definition of Terms: What is Reputation Management?

» Two books by novelist Daniel Defoe – *Moll Flanders* (1722) and *Robinson Crusoe* (1719) teach us about the world of reputation management. Essentially they show us that reputation is what other people think of us – i.e. it is based on external perceptions and conventions.

» Correctly determining your own corporate culture is vital. A useful way of segmenting your company is to use the solidarity/sociability criteria put forward by academics Goffee and Jones.

» Key audiences with whom you can communicate are best categorized into "clusters," such as business partners. This will help plan both the messages you want to get to them and the channels you use to deliver these messages.

» There are a number of well-formed "disciplines" for reputation management – practiced largely by the agency business: e.g. issues management or public affairs.

A brief look at novelist Daniel Defoe's two most famous works, *Moll Flanders* (1722) and *Robinson Crusoe* (1719), could serve as a useful entry point to the world of reputation management.

First, a condensed version of Moll Flanders' colorful biography: She

> "was Born in Newgate, and during a Life of continu'd Variety for Threescore Years, besides her Childhood, was Twelve Year a Whore, five times a Wife (whereof once to her own Brother), Twelve Year a Thief, Eight Year a Transported Felon in Virginia, at last grew Rich, liv'd Honest, and died a Penitent."

The eponymous Moll was very concerned with the preservation of her reputation – this was key not only to her success in seventeenth-century English society, but also to her very survival. Her reputation as a single woman was based on her birth status (the social order over which she had no control), her "breeding" (education, manners, "sensibility" – over which she had some control), and her ability to attract the right kind of man (at which she was pretty skilful).

An early learning point of this book is that "reputation" is a social or external convention. It is not based on what we ourselves think it is (or even ought to be). It is based on external perceptions and values. Like Moll, a corporation can seek to rise above the realities of its origin, heritage, or baggage. But also (like Moll) it needs to have a level of honesty and self-awareness of its current standing in order to be able to do so successfully.

I will now turn to that other work which has inspired many a young reader – *Robinson Crusoe*. Unlike Moll, Crusoe, when ship-wrecked on the island, did not need to worry about managing his reputation – because he went to a place where his status and conventions had no currency. The island was an environment in which Crusoe had to learn a new pecking order – and he was only nominally its master. More importantly, as he was alone on the island, the concept of reputation and hence its management was redundant. Again, "reputation" is a social or relational convention. Crusoe did not have a "society" on the island with whom he could relate. It was only when Man Friday came on the scene that he was presented with the opportunity of both relating to another human being, and establishing a master–servant rapport. At this juncture in the book the issue of "how" he was perceived by Man Friday (and hence his reputation) enters the equation.

REPUTATION IS OTHER PEOPLE

So, here is at least a partial definition. A corporation's reputation is what others think it is. More importantly, it is based not just on external perceptions, but on the behavior which is supported by these perceptions. In other words, if a corporation has a reputation for being a late payer, this only becomes an issue to be managed if it results in behavioral change by an important other (audience). For example, a key supplier choosing not to do business with you.

Corporate communications should be based on what makes an organization tick and an awareness of what the business is trying to achieve (business objective).

Sadly, most attempts at reputation management start off with little knowledge of how the business objective is being served by the activity – and with an idealized version of where the company wants to be. This can lead to bland, sanitized, and ultimately irrelevant acts of corporate communication, which we see all around us each day.

So reputation management needs to be based on a sound assessment of one's operating context *but also* on what makes it tick internally. Reputation management is not to be confused with customer relationship marketing. Reputation management is much broader and includes sets of audiences who may not have any direct commercial relationship with the business (e.g. client/supplier) but who still have a stake in the company. In this sense, a local government department would not have a direct commercial relationship with your business, but it is still key to the health of your business – particularly when it comes to planning permission for expansion of a facility, for example (see Chapter 10).

WHAT MAKES YOUR ORGANIZATION TICK?

Academics Rob Goffee and Gareth Jones have presented a way for managers to chart where their organizations stand with regard to two main criteria: sociability and solidarity. Sociability is "a measure of friendliness among members of a community. People do kind things for each other because they want to – no strings attached."

By contrast, "solidarity is based not so much on the heart as the mind. These relationships are based on common tasks ... and clearly understood shared goals that benefit all the involved parties, whether they personally like each other or not."[1]

Using these principles, Goffee and Jones have divided organizations into four main types: networked, communal, fragmented, and mercenary – see Fig. 2.1.

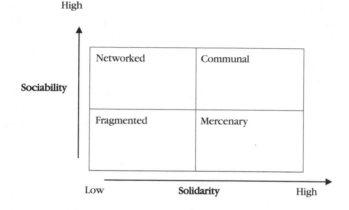

Fig. 2.1 Four types of organization.

So, for example, a technology company that aims to build and market an innovation might be a mercenary organization – it will not have much in the way of mutual support networks within the business, but will have strong teams driven towards common business goals. The top right-hand quadrant (communal) is where many organizations aspire to be (Hewlett-Packard is an example). The authors warn communal organizations to beware of smugness and complacency.

SO WHERE DO YOU START?

In finding an effective starting point for corporate communications, managers should remember that the whole organization (salespeople, call-center operators, reception, security, accounts, engineers, and so on) communicates values every day to a vast network of audiences.

In the old economy, there were only a few points of contact regulating information between the inside and outside of the organization, such as media spokespeople, analyst liaison officers, and personnel managers. In fact, the neat distinction between what lies inside and outside an organization is now becoming more difficult to make.

The proliferation of the Internet, e-mail, and supplier portals makes it easier for the outside world to interact continuously with people.

Perhaps it is of more value to think of the organization surrounded by clusters of interested parties (which we can call audiences) – see Fig. 2.2.

Specifically, the audiences can be divided up as follows.

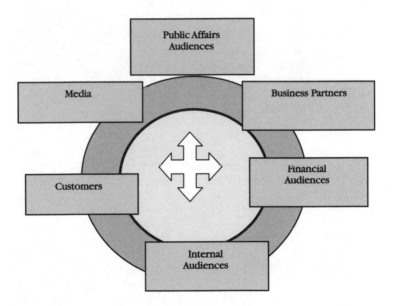

Fig. 2.2   The 360° company.

TYPES OF AUDIENCE

Public affairs audiences

» Government and politicians.
» Regulatory bodies:
  » health authorities
  » import authorities
  » local authorities.
» The industry:
  » trade associations
  » competitors.
» Non governmental organizations (NGOs)/activist groups.
» Academic organizations – schools, colleges and business schools.
» Local communities.

Media

» Local media.
» National media.
» International media.

Internal audiences

» Employees.
» Trade unions.
» Potential recruits.

Business partners

» Franchisees.
» Distributors.
» Marketing partners.
» Suppliers.

Financial audiences

» Analysts.
» Investors.
» Shareholders.

> **Customers**
> » Existing customers.
> » Potential customers.

The management of these audiences' perception of you (the business) has segmented into a number of broad disciplines – which we can briefly introduce here.

Issues management

"Issues" are defined as debates of current/potential public interest which might impact on corporate or brand reputation. They can positively and negatively affect the business. For example, biotechnology, competition policy, and healthy eating are all subjects which could have either a positive or negative impact on a business in the food industry.

   Good issues management will:

» evaluate and understand existing and/or emerging debates of relevance to the company's business; and
» develop positions and action plans consistent with its business priorities.

So back to Robinson Crusoe: a potential "issue" for Crusoe would be that of "equality" with Man Friday. If there were a "debate" beginning to rage on the island about the rectitude of Man Friday working for free for this white representative of colonial power, then it certainly would begin to impact on their working relationship and the level of service Crusoe could expect to receive. See also the Mobil Oil "op-eds" in Chapter 3.

Issues management targets

All audiences will be targets for issues management, but particularly important are "public affairs audiences," specifically NGOs/activist groups.

» *Issues management done well*: Unilever (owner of Persil, Best Foods, and Ben & Jerry's) saw the commercial leverage in growing concern for healthy living – and in particular lowering cholesterol levels. Today it is has a multibillion dollar low-fat margarine business (Flora/Becel/Take Control).

» *Issues management done badly*: Nike miscalculated the level of public and NGO concern about its low pay and conditions in the developing world facilities which made its footwear (specifically Vietnam and Indonesia). This affected sales.

Public affairs

Public affairs is closely related to issues management. Public affairs helps you develop relationships with key audiences such as government, NGOs (e.g. Greenpeace), industry groups, and local communities. For example, the public affairs process will help you:

» identify what audiences are relevant to a particular issue (e.g. the introduction of novel foods); and
» facilitate a program whereby these audiences gain a good understanding of business.

Public affairs is defined as relations with those audiences responsible for creating policy or regulation impacting on, or that contribute to, that process (e.g. government, NGOs, industry groups, academics, and so forth).

Public affairs helps you develop relationships with key audiences such as those mentioned above. It will also set in action a relationship-building program. When a particular "issue" then emerges – such as a debate on a business having an unfairly dominant position in a given marketplace – the issues management process will set in action a plan whereby the company business agenda is adequately communicated to the relevant parties.

Public affairs targets

See the 360° company chart in Fig. 2.2.

» *Public affairs done well*: British Petroleum worked cleverly with US government and non-governmental organizations on the subject of climate control and finding sustainable solutions for energy production. It has put plenty of space between itself and the competition

in terms of reputation as well as profit: today it is one of the world's most profitable companies, with a $15bn annual profit.
» *Public affairs done badly*: Microsoft, although adept at technology development, proved fairly naïve when dealing with the corridors of power at Washington and bringing down federal anti-trust actions on its back. It is now learning and hoping to try out its new-found skills on a potentially more sympathetic US Republican government.

Crisis management

Crisis management is also closely allied to issues management. A crisis is defined as: a *risk* to the company's people and/or assets which *threatens* the brand or corporate reputation and *disrupts* normal business activity and has the potential to *attract* widespread adverse attention.

Crisis management targets

Crisis management targets depend on the crisis, but typically they are media, customers, financial, and business partners.

» *Crisis management done well*: in June 1993, a Seattle family discovered a syringe in a can of Pepsi. Within 12 hours, another syringe had turned up in a can of Pepsi. Within 96 hours, Pepsi cans and syringes had become the top news story in the US; more syringes continued to appear. See also the Johnson & Johnson tylenol case in Chapter 3. It turned out that the syringes were part of a hoax in order to extort money from the company. Pepsi managed public and trade confidence immaculately – and although there was a short-term loss of $25mn in sales the brand quickly recovered.
» *Crisis management done badly*: Coca-Cola was forced to recall and destroy millions of cans and bottles from France, Belgium, and other European countries when hundreds of people fell ill after consuming the soft drink. That led to a brief sales ban which hurt profits. Chairman and CEO Doug Ivester traveled to Europe to try to address the problem, but it was too late and he soon lost his job.

Media relations

Most companies these days have a press function, usually supplemented by an external agency. The media is continuing to have a greater impact on how we view companies. This in turn necessitates better and more sophisticated media management.

We also have a series of discrete disciplines targeting distinct audiences: financial communications (targeting analysts, stockholders, and so forth), change communication (targeting employees), and community relations (targeting local communities and action groups).

KEY LEARNING POINTS

» A corporation can seek to rise above the realities of its origin, heritage, or baggage.

» Reputation is based on external perceptions and conventions.

» Work out what makes your company tick – based on the elements of solidarity and sociability.

» Reputation management can be organized around clusters of audiences: "community," "market," "organization" and "owners."

» Techniques in reputation management – e.g. public affairs – are loosely based on these clusters.

NOTES

1 Quoted in Goffee, R. & Jones, G. *The Character of a Corporation: How Your Company's Culture Can Make or Break Your Business*. HarperCollins Business, New York.

The Evolution of Reputation Management

» Reputation management, as a formal exercise, really only took off at the beginning of the last century.
» American journalist Ivy Lee Ladbetter established some early principles: "supply prompt and accurate information concerning subjects which it is of interest and value to the public to know about."
» Roosevelt, Ford, and Insull were all natural born communicators.
» Large corporates have led the way in good corporate reputation management: AT&T, Mobil Oil (issues management), and Johnson & Johnson (crisis management).

FOBBING OFF THE COMPETITION

In the late 19th century, Adolphus Busch, operating out of St. Louis in the US mid-west, launched what has become the world's biggest selling beer – Budweiser. Today that brand alone commands some 5% of the total beer market.

Busch laid down not only the foundations for strong product and brand development – he also worked on creating a network of business stakeholders. As the business was much later to claim: "making friends is our business."

Part of this business success lay in the vision to create first a truly national beer brand (hitherto beers were all local), and then toward the latter end of the 20th century a truly international beer brand. The corporate logo featured what is termed the "A & Eagle" – an eagle resting on the bridge of the letter "A."

Busch had a special one designed as a fob for his pocketwatch – made from some 14 parts and featuring semi-precious stones. The whole ensemble was very eye catching. When on business, the A & Eagle fob attracted comment and admiration from the other businesspeople with whom Adolphus liaised. So at a cosmetic level, Adolphus was already pushing the corporate logo and the heritage (the eagle carried regal as well as US patriotic overtones).

Adolphus was operating at more than one level. Quite often, when complimented on the fob, Adolphus would magnanimously donate it to the other party, who would wear it with pride. This perpetuated the corporate logo and marked out a discreet club of stakeholders: the "friends" of Adolphus were clearly demarcated. Of course, Adolphus had many of these fobs made up and would have the next one in place ready to donate it to the next admiring (relevant) person.

THERE'S A BEAR IN THE AIR

One of the most powerful and effective (non-product) symbols created was that of Smokey the bear, first utilized by the US forest service in 1944. The aim of the bear was to prevent forest fires and was the brainchild of a group of foresters together with the advertising council. The bear won out over other forest creatures because of its human-like posture and the universality of its appeal. The use and subsequent success of the bear might appear deceptively simple, but essentially what was going on was a sophisticated branding process. Remember product and brand marketing was still in its infancy.

What the foresters were actually branding was not a tangible commodity, such as coffee or wheat flour, but *good practice*. This is, of course, quite an abstract process and open to interpretation. The campaign worked because it concretized/personalized good practice (the bear) and kept the message positive (looking after Smokey's habitat) rather than negative (don't do this; don't do that . . .).

Finally, through the right choice of symbol, it maximized the range of the message's appeal. So while Adolphus' corporate branding was discreet, targeted, and exclusive; Smokey was broad-ranging and inclusive.

REPUTATION MANAGEMENT AS A BUSINESS

The more formal practice of public relations (as a business) was born in times of pressurized media scrutiny on some major US corporates.

American journalist Ivy Lee Ladbetter initially handled PR for the anthracite coal industry and the Pennsylvania railroad. In establishing some principles of this work (which was essentially media relations) he claimed to:

"supply prompt and accurate information concerning subjects which it is of interest and value to the public to know about."

Of course this was just a version of the journalist's remit, which is, according to *Brill's Content*, the US magazine that monitors the media, concerned with:

» accuracy – stories should be true;
» labeling and sourcing – information should be clear and unnamed sources labeled as such; and
» conflicts of interest – content should be free of any motive "other than informing its consumers."

In 1906 Ladbetter was hired to represent George F. Parker and his associates in the coal strike of that year. Within this campaign Ladbetter issued a "Declaration of Principles," which was extremely influential in the field of public relations. As Eric Goldman observed, this declaration marked the emergence of a second stage of public relations. The public, who up to that point had been had been ignored and fooled, now needed to be informed.

Ladbetter's famous declaration was mailed to all city editors:

"This is not a secret press bureau. All our work is done in the open. We aim to supply news. This is not an advertising agency; if you think any of our matter ought properly to go to your business office, do not use it. Our matter is accurate. Further details on any subject treated will be supplied promptly, and any editor will be assisted most cheerfully in verifying directly any statement of fact ... In brief, our plan is, frankly and openly, on behalf of business concerns and public institutions, to supply to the press and public of the United States prompt and accurate information concerning subjects which it is of value and interest to the public to know about."

This open approach was used by Ladbetter in the anthracite coal strike – new channels of information were open as Ladbetter provided reports to reporters on developments of the strike after meetings. Ladbetter, by giving out these reports, was one of the first to use "press releases."

OTHER EARLY PIONEERS IN THE ART OF REPUTATION MANAGEMENT

Theodore Roosevelt

Roosevelt was a talented president as regards publicity and used this talent to his political advantage. It has been said that Roosevelt ruled America from the front pages of newspapers. On coming to power, Roosevelt came to an understanding with the press, as he "knew the value and potent influence of a news paragraph written as he wanted it written and disseminated through the proper influential channels" (quote from veteran reporter David S. Barry[1]). Roosevelt's conservation policies in the government's first large-scale publicity program saved much of America's resources from gross exploitation. He knew how to create a story so that it would get maximum attention, and his enemies had to develop similar tactics. Roosevelt exploited the news media and established a new form of presidential leadership in the process.

Henry Ford

David Lewis, who wrote about Henry Ford and his public relations techniques, states "The industrialist is revealed ... as perhaps the most astute self-advisor in the whole history of a land that has produced its full share of promoters and showmen."[2] From as early as 1908, Ford developed public relations within the automobile industry. He sought publicity, which was not the norm at this time as businesses wanted to stay as far from the public eye as possible. This may show why Ford was so successful compared with the competition.

Samuel Insull

Insull, a businessman who in the late 1890s relied on sophisticated sales strategies for his Chicago Edison Company, also cut charges to increase the use of electricity. In 1901, he created an advertising department to deal with his messages to the public, and in 1902 built a demonstration "electric cottage," and in 1903 started the *Electric City*, an external community publication, "to gain understanding and good will" in Chicago. In 1909, Insull began using films for PR uses and was possibly the first to do this. In 1912, he employed "bill stuffers" and later used these for political messages. Insull knew that "those identified with an institution are the prime determinants of its public reputation."[3]

Although government relations in the UK can be traced back some 200 years, the UK and rest of Europe lagged behind the US in terms of the growth of the consultancy business.

Between the two world wars (i.e. the 1920s and 1930s) there was a boom in the availability of consumer products – e.g. radios, automobiles – which in turn fed a hungry media. This saw the development of some "in-house" capacity to churn out a healthy supply of material that became known as "advertorial" (sales promotional material dressed up as editorial copy).

After the Second World War, many who had been dutifully employed in the art of propaganda looked to apply their well-honed skills to more explicitly commercial ends. (Interestingly, in the 17th century the Catholic Church created the word "propaganda" with its *congregatio de propaganda fide* which means "congregation for propagating the faith.")

We now turn our attention to more recent times.

MANAGING REPUTATION INTERNALLY

AT&T

An example of a major organizational reshuffle came about in the early 1980s with the court-ordered split-up of the Bell system. AT&T, the world's largest company, which dominated America's communications industry, split into eight separate companies to form AT&T and seven regional companies.

AT&T needed to change not only because of legal obligations, which it fought against, but also because it needed to take this company that employed one million people and develop a new strategy to meet the new evolving technical America. AT&T gave in to the inevitable break-up of the company and decided to use it to its advantage with advertisements at the time announcing "we've been working to make the biggest change in our lives a small change in yours."

To see why a company like AT&T can make a success of a major upheaval like its court-ordered break-up we need to take a look at its public relations philosophy. AT&T has traditionally had great pioneers managing social change. Arthur Page became vice-president of AT&T in 1927 and from the outset Page established that he would have an input to policy and that the company's performance would be a result of its reputation. We see here what Page meant:

> "All business in a democratic country begins with public permission and exists by public approval. If that be true, it follows that business should be cheerfully willing to tell the public what its policies are, what it is doing and what it happens to do. This seems practically a duty."[4]

In his 20 years with AT&T Page formulated a strategy of integrated public relations theory and practice in the Bell system and paved the way for a new company that would lead worldwide communications.

Page had a society founded in his name in 1983 when AT&T anticipated their break-up. The Arthur Page Society is "committed to the belief that public relations as a function of executive management is central to the success of the corporation." According to the society Page practiced six principles while at AT&T that are now known as "the Arthur W. Page principles."

"1. TELL THE TRUTH. Let the public know what's happening and provide an accurate picture of the company's character, ideals and principles.

2. PROVE IT WITH ACTION. Public perception of an organization is determined ninety percent by doing and ten percent by talking.

3. LISTEN TO THE CUSTOMER. To serve the company well, understand what the public wants and needs. Keep top decision-makers and other employees informed about public reaction to company products, policies and practices.

4. MANAGE FOR TOMORROW. Anticipate public reaction and eliminate practices that create difficulties. Generate goodwill.

5. CONDUCT PUBLIC RELATIONS AS IF THE WHOLE COMPANY DEPENDS ON IT. Corporate relations is a management function. No corporate strategy should be implemented without considering its impact on the public. The public relations professional is a policy-maker capable of handling a wide range of corporate communications activities.

6. REMAIN CALM, PATIENT AND GOOD HUMORED. Lay the groundwork for public relations miracles with consistent, calm and reasoned attention to information and contacts. When a crisis arises, remember that cool heads communicate best."

By the 1990s, AT&T with their seven regional companies had established their product lines well beyond the original "telephone company," manufacturing computers, entering publishing, and becoming leaders in all forms of communication. AT&T adapted and adjusted itself from a telephone company to a major player in a new digital, wireless, and multimedia environment. Long-time AT&T consultant Chester Burger, on recalling how the company succeeded with their split, states that in "the early 80s there were 1,700 full-time PR executives within the company with a budget of some $170mn" and AT&T's public relations strategy was to defend the company as an historic monopoly. Burger claims that:

"1. Public relations strategy can't overcome broad social factors. 2. It is easy to convince yourself that corporate self-interest coincides with the public interest and 3. technology is changing the world."[5]

ISSUES-BASED ADVERTORIAL

One of the most dramatic uses of issues advertising has been that of Mobil Oil's "op-eds" which first appeared on October 19, 1970. The *New York Times* introduced a second editorial page facing the original one and offered a quarter of the new page as space for image advertising. These opinion editorials were placed in the *New York Times* as well as the *Washington Post* and other periodicals. The "op-eds" cover all manner of topics not necessarily to do with the oil industry, including economic, political, and social issues important to the consumer and the company. It was Mobil's objective to encourage thought and dialogue by informing the public about the oil industry while explaining Mobil's views on key issues of the day and by presenting responsible policy proposals. While these public issues may seem outside the corporate image, in a Harris survey in 1976 on how the American public regarded 40 corporations, including 7 oil companies, Mobil came out well and was seen as the industry's pacesetter on 19 out of 21 issues set out in the survey. These "op-eds" have been a great success for Mobil Oil and continue to run in the *New York Times* and other publications today.

The 1980s introduced a new era of public relations and corporate social responsibility. A seminal moment occurred when healthcare giant Johnson & Johnson was faced with one of the seminal moments in its corporate history in its classic handling of the tylenol poisonings in 1983. This was an event which was to transform the need to manage one's reputation at a corporate level from being the occasional luxury of Fortune 500 players to being a necessity.

The fundamental *reason* why the handling of this crisis was not an accident of fortune can be seen in the Johnson & Johnson "Credo." General Robert Wood Johnson, who guided Johnson & Johnson from a small, family-owned business to a worldwide enterprise, wrote the Credo in 1943. It consisted of a one-page document that put customers first, and stockholders last, and was a refreshing approach to the management of a business.

> We believe our first responsibility is to the doctors, nurses and patients, to mothers and fathers and all others who use our products and services. In meeting their needs everything we do must be of high quality. We must constantly strive to reduce our costs in order to maintain reasonable prices. Customers' orders must be serviced promptly and accurately. Our suppliers and distributors must have an opportunity to make a fair profit.

The Credo allows the company to respond swiftly, consistently, and altruistically. For the first time, the world could see that open and frank dealings between a company and its stakeholders in times of extreme difficulty could ultimately be good for business.

It could be argued that this same approach (swift, consistent, and altruistic) could also be of value when in non-crisis circumstances. The Body Shop's successful corporate history is testimony to this.

KEY LEARNING POINTS

» Reputation management can be mass market or discreet. You just need to be able to define who are your key audiences.
» Six points advocated by former vice-president of AT&T, Arthur Page:
  1 Tell the truth.
  2 Prove it with action.
  3 Listen to the customer.
  4 Manage for tomorrow.

5 Conduct public relations as if the whole company depends on it.
6 Remain calm, patient, and good humored.

NOTES

1 Quoted in Cutlip, S.M., Center, A.H. & Broom, G.M. (2000) *Effective Public Relations* (8th edn). Prentice Hall, Englewood Cliffs, NJ.
2 Lewis, D.L. (1976) *The Public Image of Henry Ford: An American Hero And His Company*. Wayne State University Press, Detroit.
3 Lewis, D.L. (1976) *The Public Image of Henry Ford: An American Hero And His Company*. Wayne State University Press, Detroit.
4 Griswold, G. Jr (1967) "How AT&T public policies developed." *Public Relations Quarterly*, **12** (Fall).
5 Burger, C. (1997) "Last word: when public relations fails." *Strategist*, **3**(3).

The E-Dimension

» The ability to circumvent traditional knowledge bases (e.g. medical) will pose a real problem for corporations to manage. This can be seen in many medical chat rooms where victims canvas for allies, which could ultimately result in a class-action suit against a "culprit" corporation.

» Hollywood has also been exposed by ain't-it-cool-news.com when it tries to tailor its endings to suit popular tastes – or at least avoid a commercial flop.

» Corporations simply cannot use the Internet as another "channel" because the nature of the Web is anarchic and will not be tamed and oriented for commercial ends so easily. It thrives on the "porno-graphic," i.e. that which lies outside acceptable social norms.

» The social conventions which e-mail is overturning (i.e. flattening hierarchies) can be good for business – but we are in danger of swamping each other with information of relatively low value.

"Over time, tension will grow, pitting the global world of digital commerce and online society against the more local worlds of traditional governments and of people who aren't part of the 'brave new world.'"

Esther Dyson[1]

Dyson frames the fight in regulatory terms. But regulation comes after the dust has settled. Regulation consolidates the position of the winner. The winner is still far from clear. In this chapter we look at how the digital age both enables and conflicts with the advancement of a corporate reputation. In fact it boils down to information management. If you do not manage information pertinent to how key audiences may perceive you – then your reputation management systems will be lost.

Up until now much discussion about information management has focused on how the corporation can enhance performance using new technologies (Federal Express – parcel tracking using the Internet); or on product innovation (Mondex Electronic Purse – electronic cash); or on how new competitors have changed the rules of the game and overturned dominant players (Amazon.com – Internet book shop).

But the real impact of new technology on the corporation promises to be more fundamental as it will involve a profound struggle. This battle will be between those who have power (the corporation) and those who have increasing access to information, thereby dissipating that power. The opponents reside outside the corporate boundary: consumers, potential consumers, trade customers, shareholders, competitors, regulators, and activists.

The cozy coterie which the average multimillion-dollar corporation can command (lobbyists, lawyers, scientists, spin-doctors, trade associations) is threatened in this "brave new world." The cohesive, consistent voice and face of the corporation is threatened in the digital world and with it the power which it has so carefully nurtured and enhanced.

In many respects, the cyber-age poses a greater threat to corporate reputations than those other antagonists such as the activist groups – because the threat is amorphous. The threat poses a challenge not only for the corporation but also for other "fixed" institutions of power which "represent," i.e. have been invested with power by others to represent interests on their behalf, e.g. government. The falling trust or interest in government is also visible in the rise of the activist group.

The reason why a pressure group such as Greenpeace is able to command such attention and goodwill among its membership is that it occupies a space in the public trust zone vacated by government.

Greenpeace is therefore *invested* with some power to *represent* interests and there is a consequent falling off of power within the government. As the German author Heiden remarked: "Unused power slips imperceptibly into the hands of another."[2]

All around us in the age of information there is a dissipation in the traditional modes of representation. This has direct implications for the corporate–public transaction. Let's look at a few situations where consumers (helped by technology) choose new ways of representing *their own* interests – usually at the expense of another's reputation.

WHEN DOES THE REVOLUTION START WITH THE MONARCHY?

Hamel's line suggests that change is always bottom or peripherally driven, never a top-down central initiative. In the same way, the overturn of corporate dominance will not be driven from within but from without. The individual, through his or her ability to form meaningful informal alliances, is already presenting strong and direct challenges to the corporation.

But it is now clear that the ability of the individual to access information pertinent to his or her own interest is turning the tables.

FORMING INFORMAL ALLIANCES: AN INTERNET EXAMPLE

The Internet enables disparate sets of audiences to find each other, exchange information, and perhaps agree mutual agendas. These are agendas which can be antagonistic to the business. For example, let's look at the area of health, an area particularly busy on the Web. Using wbs.net one can visit the personal sites of, and correspond directly with, users with equivalent agendas. Here is a sample from a message board:

4EVER A STUDENT

Interested in cardiology & neonatology.

92163

I am interested in hearing from those with hypothyroidism.

ACUTE ASS

Surgical first assistant.

BEEESS

I am looking for individuals who have become ill from exposure to the weedkiller "Roundup."

BJL150

I like to keep informed of new medical information.

CHEMORN

I'm an oncology nurse, and mum, and parrot-head!

COMMANDER – GENERAL ADAM

I am a chronic asthmatic who enjoys supporting others with respiratory illnesses.

CURIOUS THE MIGHTY

Emergency Department RN/manager.

CWALL12

I am a registered dietician specializing in wellness, diabetes, renal nutrition.

The Web provides the user with the ability to access information and thereby gain a wealth of information about his/her own condition. It also allows each user to form and be part of a "web" of alliances and information exchanges which can form nodal points outside of and perhaps even antagonistic to the interest of business.

Remember BeeEss?

"I am looking for individuals who have become ill from exposure to the weedkiller 'Roundup.'"

BeeEss doesn't just want to share information on a health basis. It is not absurd to suppose that if the response to BeeEss' message was strong, some formal (perhaps legal) representation to Monsanto (the manufacturers of Roundup) might ensue.

This type of information and information network now available so cheaply to the individual would never have been possible using traditional forms of research (private detectives, medical searches, trawls of relevant journals) because of time, financial, and educational limitations on the individual.

THE CORPORATE CHALLENGE

As we saw, the healthcare industry is an accessible sector in which it is easy to view how a company's reputation (medical/professional/ethical) might be challenged effectively and easily through the collection and positioning of information sourced on the Web. This also holds true for the many other commercial spheres.

LET'S GO TO HOLLYWOOD

Take the Hollywood film industry, a powerful and market-led sector which is being threatened by Harry Knowles, a single, overweight film-buff who posts film reviews from his bedroom in Austin, Texas. The site is called www.ain't-it-cool-news.com and seeks to give advance warning on whether an upcoming film release is good or not. It its own words:

"Ain't It Cool News is a Harry Knowles production bringing you the latest in movie, TV, comic and other coolness that's got Hollywood's panties in a bunch."

As Harry describes his own growing fame/infamy, so also the network of informal alliances begin to grow around him:

> "Wow, here ya are! Well my little site keeps on growing, much to my shock. As you will find I attempt to cover all stages of development of the films that you and I look forward to, without the 'studio line' clouding our judgment.
>
> "This site works with the help of people like you. Now everyone has a chance to be a 'spy,' because inevitably at some point there will be a moment where Hollywood enters your life, before it enters ours. If you see something filming, a trailer, an advance screening or something I can't even imagine. If you read a script, hear something from behind the scenes . . .
>
> "Well let me know. I try to cover it all, and you, your neighbors, boss, or even the local weatherman . . . well y'all make this site special. It's your eyes, ears and opinions, well . . . we're making a difference. Also we do cover the 'uncool' films, we warn each other of the Hollywood powered Nuclear Bombs, and the super cool products."

Note the use of the word "spy" Harry is openly exhorting a show of subversion to the multibillion-dollar Hollywood industry, an industry which test markets its products (particularly their endings) on focus groups, adapting the final product to consumer needs.

Harry's warnings to site users have made him a target of Hollywood attention and vitriol.

Such is the enormous investment in films that a few failures can threaten the financial health of the studio. This makes powerful media such as 'Ain't It Cool News' absolutely key in determining how the weathervane of popular opinion will swing. Harry has been keen to distance himself from the commercial interests which might influence the more mainstream reviewers. He stresses that the banner advertising in his site is unsolicited, does not influence him, and has the benefit of keeping the site free of charge to users.

TECHNOLOGY AND INTERNAL REPUTATION MANAGEMENT

History shows that business did not start the Web, but business is now desperately trying to catch up and to exploit its potential. Yet intranets (internal corporate sites) still lag behind the sophistication of Internet sites. If you are looking for the agent in the technology revolution, it will probably be somewhere outside the corporate boundary. The Internet is still an outsider's paradise – an anarchist's dream.

Indeed, the Internet remains contrarian. The huge and growing cyber-community is made up of a proliferating network of alliances which have little real care for the business. Indeed, they are theoretically opposed to powerful bodies – government, religious institutions, corporations, etc. In the case of www.ain't-it-cool-news.com, Harry Knowles seeks to provide his audience with honest and unadulterated reviews, free from the influences of the Hollywood marketing machine.

There is an ongoing battle. On one side there are those who see technology as a means of subverting or circumventing the official channels (bolstered by the Internet's relative freedom from libel laws). They argue that they are entitled to as much information about the world around them as possible and free of charge. The Web is the key tool to help them make that happen. It also allows them to share that information with a new global community with similar interests without constraint.

These are the net-heads who champion freedom of speech, privacy, market democratization, and the radical democracy. The Web environment has up until now had, and perhaps always will have, an air of the unofficial. This is manifest most simply in the sense that there is very little *original* corporate material produced for the Web.

Most of the content of corporate sites has been tailored electronic versions of materials which have previously existed in different formats. Companies, particularly in Europe, are still struggling to find the right tone of voice for their Websites. This is partly due to the newness of the medium and the requirement to replace static one-directional communications with dynamic interactive ones.

It has also got to do with the difficulty in reconciling the official corporate voice of the organization with the inherently anarchic and self-debunking nature of the medium. Of course, at its most tedious, the corporation tries to use the medium as an electronic shop window.

The huge amount of pornography available on the net is also testimony to the inherently secretive, alternative appeal of the medium. Pornography is that which is rejected by society. It occupies a place beyond the line of social respectability and what is considered the normal interplay between humans. Many bemoan the amount of pornography on the net and would attempt to have it cleaned up. But that is to miss the point. The *nature* of the medium is inherently pornographic. Pornography has also played a part in other revolutions. In pre-Revolution France, pornographic material denigrated the aristocracy, and Marie Antoinette in particular. It encouraged irreverence towards the ruling class. It helped undermine the existing power base. Politics, power, and pornography can be bedfellows in more ways than one. The fact remains that pornography is actually driving much of the technical innovation on the Internet – the use of streaming video and so forth.

Businesses which took years to form and build up trade, customer relations, quality assurance, and the like, see a three-year-old organization float for billions of dollars on the exchange. It doesn't make any sense in a normal business mode. Look at the speed at which Java built up a customer base, for example.

This cyber-world is pornographic, not just in the literal sense of the availability of pornography, but also in the sense that part of its function is to subvert accepted norms. In a way, the net is also inherently revolutionary. From the perspective of personal power, it can break the grip which the corporation places on you (whether you are on the inside or the outside of organization) and set you on your way to accruing personal power for yourself.

If the organization can lock the employee into a power relation by manipulating the space in which he or she operates, then the Internet displaces this spatial organization and replaces it with virtual space – the first step in liberating and empowering the individual. The Net throws power up in the air. Freed from their corporate cells, employees are able to take flight in cyberspace.

In the past, access to information came with privilege: privileged information equalled power. But the Net is no respecter of privilege. Relevance is the new arbiter. The new power base will lie with those who can establish the most relevant information base.

Indeed all the traditional power bases, not just the commercial, are threatened in the new age we are entering. Presidents and kings relied on privileged information to underpin their power. Witness what access to information about the British Royal Family has done to that institution in the past two decades.

What does this mean for businesses? Are the corporations going to be out of business? The simple answer is no. Commercial trading will continue – but the traditional means in which the organization maintains its owner value will radically alter, and technology will be one of the key factors prompting this. This is because the Net will fragment the corporate power base and hand it back to the people. It's already happening. Look at the trouble Shell found itself in when it tried to dispose of the *Brent Spar* oil platform. And again, over its operations in Nigeria. Public opinion, fuelled by access to previously privileged information, can no longer be ignored.

This Internet culture shares information and perpetuates truths and rumors. In fact it blurs the difference and treats them with equal respect. So what does this mean for business people? If you're a big time polluter or treat people – employees, customers, shareholders – badly, then you're in for a rough ride. If not, then the important lesson is about how you get things done. Without an information power base, control is no longer a viable strategy. Influence is the way forward. Persuasion is the new game. You have to persuade people to do business with you. The simplest way to do that is to offer real value.

Providing value allows you to avoid the crossfire. The new technology can help you do that. The great failure of the technological revolution so far is its failure in this area. Microsoft and others have not put enough effort into creating value for their business associates – customers – to merit loyalty. Think value, and you're halfway to making the Net work for you.

INFORMATION AND COMMUNICATION

It is astonishing to think that six or seven years ago e-mail was the preserve of the chosen few rather than a tool of the masses. Now, it is an omnipresent fact of business life. A trickle has become a deluge and, as executives with 50 daily e-mails to wade through are quick to tell you, more is not always good. At Sun Microsystems 1.5 million internal messages come and go every day. That's 120 per employee. In the information business, quantity and quality are rarely synonymous. This has prompted Larry Ellison to bemoan the "irrational distribution of data and complexity," and he warns:

> "We're putting databases in hamburger stands, branch offices, and banks – it's all a mistake. A colossal mistake, this irrational distribution of information."[3]

Signs are that the first rush of enthusiasm for e-mail may be waning. One big company in the computing industry is considering banning e-mail in the afternoon. It found that people had stopped talking to one another. MIT's William Lucas cites one amazing piece of research which found that 92% preferred e-mail to "keep someone informed" – a mere 0.8% chose face-to-face communication.[4] E-mail only fared less well in communicating personal information or if the aim was to influence, persuade, or sell an idea.

Things aren't all bad. William Lucas' research suggests that, at least, e-mail is inexpensive. In the US, Intel has calculated that each message from its 20,000 e-mail users cost four cents. In the UK, BT estimates that using e-mail on average saves the user 3.5 hours a week (an amount equivalent to £9,000 per year).

Lucas draws two conclusions. First:

> "e-mail makes organizational communications easier, faster, and more efficient."

His second conclusion is perhaps more interesting:

> "By supporting the growth of a wide variety and growing number of low intensity and informal relationships between an organization's employees and others both inside and external to the organization, e-mail is posing a new and paradoxical management challenge."

Flexible, egalitarian, and informal, e-mail challenges many of the conventions of traditional organizations where communication is carefully controlled and limited. While the medium challenges, there are few signs that flexibility, egalitarianism, and informality have been embraced.

E-mail has also accelerated another trend: information overload. Research has shown that too much information is now a major cause of stress in the workplace, leading to ill-health and the breakdown of personal relationships. The problem is exacerbated by inadequate IT training and the failure of many organizations to introduce policies and procedures for managing information.

The effects of the information glut, Lucas' report suggests, are procrastination and time wasting, the delaying of important decisions, distraction from main job responsibilities, tension between colleagues, and loss of job satisfaction. Many of those surveyed also reported that information overload caused high levels of stress resulting in illness and the breakdown of personal relationships.

But why should information suddenly present such a problem? According to Paul Waddington, marketing manager at Reuters Business Information, there are two main factors. One, he says, is the huge increase in the volume of information emanating from both within the organization and outside – from customers, suppliers, and other sources, including the media. At the same time there has been an explosion of enabling technology which people are struggling to understand. As a result, information is crashing in on us from all sides. Waddington says:

> "There used to be just internal memos and meetings, now there is e-mail, the Internet and a host of other tools to deal with. In the past people were able to develop ways of filtering information, but now there is such a flood that they can't do that anymore."[5]

Comments David Lewis:

> "Many companies are still in the dark ages when it comes to managing the flow of information, trying to communicate everything to everyone. Sometimes a manager will copy a memo to 2,000 people just to show his seniority. We also know that individuals can be targeted for a form of sabotage, where someone is deliberately singled out and flamed with information from all sides – using e-mail for example – just to make their life difficult."[6]

The recognition that information overload is a potential threat to the well-being of employees is hardly encouraging. Dr. Lewis agrees:

> "Really, it's about the interface between the human brain and technology. Information is not knowledge until it has been processed

by the human mind. A definition of knowledge is information which reduces uncertainty. But too much information actually increases uncertainty and is very stressful."[7]

According to Paul Waddington at Reuters, companies need to focus on effective information-sharing technology, rather than the indiscriminate approach many have taken so far, and create formal policies and procedures for information management. Written standards for e-mail, for example, he says, could drastically reduce the problem of junk e-mail by providing clear guidelines to the sorts of information that should be circulated and to whom. He says:

"At present it's not unusual for someone to receive 60 e-mail messages a day. Rather than them deciding which they should respond to and which to ignore, it makes sense to look at how many of those 60 should have been sent in the first place."[8]

The psychologist David Lewis also sees a pressing need for new sorts of training:

"On a personal level, people need skills for handling information. Most people have very bad reading habits, dating back to when they learned to read out loud at school. They still translate printed symbols into a voice in their head – sometimes you can even see their lips moving. That's a major block on their ability to process information. What they need now is to learn is to read in a completely different way; to ask the data a question, then skim down until they find the answer."

MANAGING REPUTATION INTERNALLY

The typical response to change within an organization during times of change is to throw more data and information at the employee. Again, remember what we said earlier: too much information actually increases uncertainty, and uncertainty is not good for business.

The digital age provides the manager with very sophisticated tools for disseminating information to a whole range of internal and external stakeholders. But the "brave new world" also opens up the company so that the distinction between outside and inside is actually blurred.

When it comes to management of reputation–this perhaps is one of the greatest challenges posed by the age of e-business.

KEY LEARNING POINTS

» The Internet is subversive in nature and loves gossip – it is still untamed by corporations.

» The Internet also enables new clusters of audiences, which can form separate sources of information about your company.

» If reputation management is, in part, information management, then the Internet can potentially upturn the existing ways in which we build and manage our corporate reputation.

» The digital revolution has resulted in a mass of information being exchanged. This does not necessarily make the task of reputation management easier. The first step is to work out which information will advance the business objective.

NOTES

1 Dyson, E. (1998) *A Design for Living in the Digital Age*. Broadway Books, New York.
2 Quoted in Crainer, S. (1997) *The Ultimate Book of Business Quotations*. Capstone Publishing, New York.
3 Quoted in Griffin, G. (1999) *Con*. Suntop Media, London.
4 Lucas, W. (1999) "Effects of e-mail on the organization." *European Management Journal*, **16**(1).
5 Quoted in Griffin, G. (1999) *Con*. Suntop Media, London.
6 Quoted in Griffin, G. (1999) *Con*. Suntop Media, London.
7 Quoted in Griffin, G. (1999) *Con*. Suntop Media, London.
8 Quoted in Griffin, G. (1999) *Con*. Suntop Media, London.

The Global Dimension

» The recent high-profile demonstrations against economic globalization need to be taken seriously by those wishing to maintain a business reputation across boundaries.

» Technology will be a key driver of globalization but consumers will need to be managed better if we are to avoid another GM fiasco, when the public got scared about a positive and harmless innovation.

» McDonald's has managed its global drive very well – particularly because it has adapted to local needs (e.g. differing menus to take account of cultural or religious differences).

» Businesses now need to be able to respond to crises speedily and internationally or else risk being peripheralized – as happened after the Guam air crash.

Recently we have seen increasingly violent public protests around the world, from Göthenburg to Genoa – that latter in which a protester was shot dead by police. The demonstrators have not been protesting about nuclear disarmament or GM foods or the environment, although it is also likely that the protesters would all have fixed views about these issues. The issue that is attracting such passionate demonstration is actually that of globalization. These are anti-global protesters and they are not going away. In fact, we can take it that for the next few years, wherever George W. Bush appears outside of the US, a nodal point in the growing web of anti-global feeling will form.

Anti-globalization has a strong bias toward green or environmental concerns (saving forests, global warming, freeing the streets). It is also providing a rubric for general anti-capitalist and pro-anarchist sentiment. Typical symbols for passive and violent protest are NikeTown and McDonald's. Of course, these anti-global protests could be just a PC (non-xenophobic) version of good old-fashioned anti-American feeling, which has a strong tradition – particularly in Europe.

There is, though, something qualitatively distinct from simply a stand against American economic imperialism in current anti-globalization protesting. It is perhaps too easy to dismiss the protesters as sets of people who have run out of other things to rail against. As trading blocs coalesce with multinationals as a prime catalyst, there are major corporate reputations at stake.

MAKE MINE A ... BOSTON STEAM

If you go back to the beer business in the 1990s, niche breweries or micro-breweries were enjoying major popularity. This was based on the premise that a micro-beer was somehow more authentic, original, and natural than a mass-produced (pasteurized) mass-market brand. Consuming an Anchor Steam was a stronger act of faith than getting wasted on Coors. There was also a fortunate synergy between the "natural" messages being championed by the environmentalists and the authenticity and naturalness of some of these micro-breweries. They somehow hearkened back to a time of skilled artisans turning out a genuine product for a modest profit to the local hinterland.

Anti-globalization contends that somehow we have lost this authentic way of life. One of the major culprits, in their view, in this loss of innocence is your faceless multinational.

Many companies such as Proctor and Gamble and Unilever are looking increasingly to the global brands and global events to showcase those brands as the way forward. This is the equivalent of turning the Marathon candy bar into Snickers everywhere and then getting it to sponsor the World Cup.

WHAT LIES BEHIND THE GLOBAL DREAM

As these global businesses and global marketers embrace the global village and dream of their respective brands competing for market share in various parts of the world – like some heady war-game – are they also aware of the deep and growing antagonism of the anti-global protesters?

This sometimes violent (and in itself quite global) uprising has intellectual underpinnings. *No Logo*[1] is a book which does not conceal its distaste of the "biggies" of global branding, e.g. Nike. In particular, it explores Nike's alleged poor treatment of workers through its third-party supplier relationships in Vietnam and Indonesia. The book argues that because of Nike's drive towards giving global branding dominance within the company, its interest in actually manufacturing the products is diminished. Again, because of the actual cost of having major sponsors such as Michael Jordan involved, it seeks to source its products as cheaply as possible.

McDonald's ran into equivalent problems after it was involved in the famous McLibel trial, when it successfully sued two protesters from London Greenpeace for handing out defamatory leaflets. Although McDonald's won the case (one of the longest in legal history) it proved a hollow victory. The judge found that there was some substance to the protesters' claims that animals used in the supply chain suffered and that McDonald's did target children with some of their advertising. Most importantly, the case did not stem but in fact enhanced the level of protest against the company.

McDonald's has had to put up with many protests against its business across the world – including retail outlets being burned.

THE ESTABLISHMENT VIEW

Moving on to what the *establishment* means by globalization and its drivers, the National Intelligence Council, a sort of in-house CIA think tank, cites one of the biggest drivers in the spread of globalization to be technology:

> "The continuing diffusion of information technology and new applications in the biotechnology field will be of particular global significance.
>
> "The integration of existing disciplines to form new ones. The integration of information technology, biotechnology, materials sciences, and nanotechnology will generate a dramatic increase in innovation.
>
> "The time between the discovery and the application of scientific advances will continue to shorten. Developments in the laboratory will reach commercial production at ever faster rates, leading to increased investments."[2]

IMPLICATIONS FOR CORPORATIONS

In the 1990s we saw how technology overhauled and debunked accepted business practice. Despite the dot.com bubble having well and truly burst, the business paradigm *has* shifted. As we have seen in Chapter 4 on the e-dimension, transparency with both consumers and customers everywhere is increasingly a precondition of successful business. This particularly comes down to price transparency which the Internet had led on. But it also embraces transparency in business practice. For example, business to business supplier portals signal the death knell to old-fashioned and cozy buyer–supplier relationships/networks based on history and friendship rather than on price and quality.

The National Intelligence Council also cites the speed to market of new technology applications. This means that consumers on the street will be confronted with a bewildering array of technology-based products and applications fighting for their share of your wallet. This is fairly innocuous if it just entails a wristwatch upon which you can see your favorite TV soap. But if the product is a result of a process involving genetic modification (GM), concerns may grow. Indeed they did so in the 1990s when (particularly in Europe and parts of Asia) the backlash against GM was virulent.

If the move toward increased globalization implies that time "between the discovery and the application of scientific advances" will shorten, the role of the modern and future corporation will also change. We can no longer rely on governments to educate on these innovations – they will be doing their best merely to regulate. We cannot rely on NGOs to champion the cause of the consumer – this would merely result in a climate of fear and suspicion. Commercial value of speed to market will see a growth in the number of "public permission" hurdles to be encountered by the technology innovators.

During the 1990s, when Monsanto was innovating its Roundup-ready soybeans that contained genuine environmental and farming benefits, it failed to clear some of these "public permission" hurdles. In fact, the company became a target for protesters as symbolizing US technology imperialism, meaning that Monsanto was exporting to Europe and the rest of the world a product which did not apparently represent any value to consumers but which potentially had lethal consumer and environmental implications.

We shall see in the case study dealing with Shell and *Brent Spar* that the NGOs do not need to scientifically prove these scare claims – merely raise the flag of skull and crossbones. This freedom to terrify the consumer is one of the great gifts of modern international NGOs. The trust they have was once accorded to governments. If business does not at least partly take responsibility for educating consumers in the real benefits of technology innovation, then we will see the GM fiasco repeated again and again and outside of biotechnology.

There is a clear role for the corporation to take a proactive stance on a number of these issues and gain consumer trust. If the modern-day multinational is to avoid becoming an easy target for the anti-global protesters, business will need to become more readily associated with solutions. These solutions can (and indeed should) be good for business. In Chapter 6 "The State of the Art" we will look at how and why business can and should get involved in solutions-based activity and maintain an eye on the bottom line. In our case studies, we also look at how a specific company, Bitor, repositioned itself as part of a solution.

CONSISTENCY IS KEY

The other challenge which globalization represents is that of consistency. No longer can a business say one thing in one part of the world and say (or do) something different elsewhere. This is what got Nike into hot water in the late 1990s with its third-party supplier relations in Vietnam. Its stance (brand proposition) was 'cool' and anti-establishment. However, campaigners (The Campaign for Labor Rights) as well as TV documentaries accused the company of decidedly uncool and establishment behavior when it came to pay and conditions for 38,000 workers in Vietnam. Interestingly, when Nike finally capitulated and improved pay and conditions, it did not result in the NGOs lessening their attacks on the company. A clear lesson for other businesses is to avoid being targeted in the first place by taking proactive and pre-emptive action.

In the 21st century, clear and consistent communication must surround and be part of effective corporate reputation management. The Internet is a vital tool in helping businesses communicate with a wide variety of interested parties. Again, though, the Internet is also part of the problem. For a company to be consistent in what it says and does, it must also be the center of the information relay. The Internet is proving to be a way in which outside audiences might seek to bypass the company and become their own centers of information. A case in point is revealed after the Guam air crash of 1997.

On the CNN Interactive message board after the Guam crash, Korean Air, the media, and the Government were all ignored as possible or credible sources of information. Some samples:

> "It is not surprising that the Korean media has quickly jumped on the 'bad weather' and 'landing system' as likely causes to this tragedy ..."
>
> *Tom Serey*
>
> "I could see the crash from my house the night it happened ... I am proud to say that the efforts of both the military and civilians here on Guam has been nothing short of amazing ..."
>
> *William H. Shaw III*

"At 3 miles from the runway, the course of the jumbo jet should be in the final approach position or on the center of the runway. So the most probable cause of the crash is due to pilot error."

mdk.vic

"I am a Captain for a major US airline ... My greatest disappointment is reserved for the hyena-like activities of your journalists mercilessly hounding the bereaved ..."

Rory Kay

The corporate reputations of tomorrow will increasingly be determined by message boards such as these. Victims, eye witnesses, experts, commentators, and gossips will all share information and opinion without the corporate blessing or involvement. Korean Air's own version of events, its own safety record, its reassurance to its customers – none of these items made it onto these message boards.

Earlier we saw how McDonald's was repeatedly a target for anti-global/anti-US protesters who were unhappy with such a potent symbol of capitalism in their neighborhood. That said, McDonald's has been spectacularly successful at getting its brand and its business into many disparate cultures and nations – all the while maintaining an equivalent if not identical consumer proposition.

GLOBAL VERSUS LOCAL: THE MCDONALD'S RECIPE FOR SUCCESSFUL GLOBAL EXPANSION

The first McDonald's restaurant opened in Illinois in 1955. Today, the company operates more than 27,000 restaurants in 120 countries worldwide. There are around 12,600 outlets in the US and key international markets are Japan and the UK. Since 1998, McDonald's has been fixing its gaze beyond the bun and nugget market with investments in other restaurant concepts, such as Chipotle Mexican Grill, Aroma coffee shops and Donatos Pizzas. In 2000, it acquired 750 Boston Market restaurants, invested in the Internet food delivery service Food.com, and announced plans for eMac Digital, a B2B (business to business) exchange for the food service industry.

McDonald's has also been successful in pushing its aggressive globalization policy in the Middle East. According to McDonald's:

"McDonald's' 1993 franchising debut in the region, in Israel, was followed by 'exponential' growth to a current tally of 240 branches dotting 'pretty much all the Gulf states' but focused principally in Saudi Arabia, Israel, Egypt, and Turkey."[3]

Key to unlocking these types of lucrative markets has been the requirement to source raw materials properly.

"Instead of taking a one-country-at-a-time approach to establishing its supply infrastructure, McDonald's simultaneously set up distribution channels for the entire region... 'That's why we are able to open about a dozen markets in an 18-month period,' citing the Golden Arches' rapid spanning of the entire Middle East from its core territories of Israel, Turkey, Egypt, and Saudi Arabia."[4]

There are a host of religious and cultural sensitivities to be managed (e.g. hal-al and kosher) and failure to manage the expectations would be disastrous for the company's expansion plans.

Specifically, McDonald's has had to adapt its menus and supply chain policy to make sure that it can comply locally. At the same time, the brand holds out a global promise to consumers. Managing these tensions successfully underpins the successful operation of the business. As McDonald's works primarily through franchisers, the careful selection and management of these stakeholders is fundamental.

Ultimately the consumer will receive his or her McDonald's experience at the hands of the franchiser. And we know that this experience counts for a whole lot more than expensive advertising and sponsorship. Managing the millions of daily McDonald's "experiences," mostly through the hands of third parties and mostly successfully, is a hallmark of the McDonald's expertise in global expansion.

KEY LEARNING POINTS

Avoiding being a symbol

Avoid your company being a target or symbol for the growing antiglobal sentiment. This is clearly easier said than done. It comes down ultimately to your corporate mindset: wanting to work and through relevant stakeholders. The Monsanto experience of the 1990s bears this out. Monsanto did not work with stakeholders in Europe and became a symbol of what was bad regarding GM. In fact the first time most people ever heard about Monsanto was in a negative context.

Be the center of key information about your company

As with Monsanto and also in the case of Korean Air, getting by-passed in the race to supply consumers with information about you and your business can be detrimental. Message boards right across the Internet are constantly pushing information and misinformation about your activities. Discriminate between what will and what will not have an impact. Correct the misinformation that will or might have an impact on your business.

Be consistent

The need to be constantly consistent between words and policy – between policy and deeds – is more of a journey than a destination. Consistency is never some place you arrive at but the will to be consistent will add a rigor and an integrity to your activities.

Educate consumers in advance of innovation

Unless business gets proactively involved, the stage will be left clear to self-interested NGOs to manage consumers' trust on their behalf. We know already where this will lead. There is little point in expensive R&D without preparing the market to receive technology-based offerings. Regulators will struggle to keep up and are not capable of inspiring the populations at large with trust.

Adapt to local needs where expedient

McDonald's adapts locally where it needs to – providing an equivalent rather than an utterly identical experience for consumers across the globe. Although it has had more than its fair share of antagonists, it still managed to open 1,800 stores in the year 2000 (the vast majority of the new restaurants were outside the US).

NOTES

1 Klein, N. (2001) *No Logo*. Flamingo, London.
2 For a study, see: www.odci.gov/cia/publications/globaltrends2015
3 *Nations-Restaurant-News*, **32**(7), February 16, (1998).
4 *Nations-Restaurant-News*, **32**(7), February 16, (1998).

The State of the Art

» Corporations who engage in environmental issues either for "fad" reasons or because it might inoculate them against NGO attack are being accused of "greenwashing."

» "Corporate branding" and "corporate social responsibility" are two current terms which summarize the main thrust of corporate reputation management thinking.

» CSR needs to exist as practice rather than mere policy, as evident in the Marine Stewardship Council initiative begun by Unilever and WWF.

» Within the agency world, viral marketing (the ability to create word-of-mouth positive opinion) ought to be the real driver of new business – but many struggle to achieve real excellence in this area.

Reputation management – particularly when applied to corporations – is still young. Excitingly, many of the new and different ways in which a company can manage its relationships – and by extension, its role in society – are new.

Of course many have been arguing over the role of the corporation within society for some time. On one hand you have those who propose that a company is just a vehicle for delivering owner value – include shareholders as owners here. There are others such as Sumantra Ghoshal who believe that the corporation is one of the primary sources of value in our society – providing wealth and structure as well as goods and services.

There has also been a widespread acknowledgment that the resources which are consumed by society at large are finite. Fossil fuels, water, soil, and energy are all valuable commodities and should be used discriminately. The power failures in California during 2001 serve only to remind us all of this. Nuclear technology, which was going to deliver electricity too cheap to meter, has really been a failure. Ironically, the biggest threat we face environmentally today is not from another Chernobyl but from global warming – to which the burning of traditional fossil fuels is a major contributor.

There are two fundamental ways in which corporations can react to the increasing set of social functions with which they are being expected to engage.

First, they can see these "debates" as a fad or a trend. They may dedicate some internal resource to engaging in debates about such things as water sustainability. They would see such activity as "good for the image." Ultimately they have little intention of changing their business behavior as a result of these debates. NGOs have realized this and have termed such passive engagement in environmental debates as "greenwashing." They feel frustrated that their agenda is not really being engaged with. From the outside in, it is very hard in the short term to differentiate between companies which are sincere and those which are not when it comes to active engagement with these issues. Time will tell – and altered business behavior will be the primary criterion of judgment.

Companies which fall into this first category are mistakenly short-termist. You do not have to be a sandal-wearing tree hugger to realize that if you do not engage in these social value debates in a sincere fashion, you will undermine your company's and perhaps your industry sector's credibility. Remember, if debate is an information transaction between you and a set of audiences, then credibility is your currency. The words and deeds may be perfect – but if your credibility is low then what is the point?

I have noted the tobacco industry's attempts to embrace corporate social responsibility (CSR) platforms. Indeed I have been asked to look at CSR platforms for them myself.

I suppose that if your products cause millions of our fellow humans to die in agony each year, then you need to try and show something on the credit side. But surely the credibility of these firms is low? Only an active acknowledgment of the harm that they have caused – and an action plan to stop so doing – could restore this credibility.

British Petroleum was the first in the oil industry to acknowledge the threat of global warming and the fact that the oil industry was a major culprit. This first step was then followed by a personal crusade led by its chief John Browne to alter business behavior (within BP as well as within the industry) so as to align it with the new stance.

This leads us on to the second reaction to the new social demands being made on corporations: that of a sincere realization not only that something needs to be done, but that they have a role to play within these debates. However, we need to add a "enlightened self-interest" angle. This new stance needs to "sell more beer." This means that you need to align your business objective with this debate. If you do not do so, then the activity will inevitably fall into the category of image management and slip down the priority pole.

SELF-ENLIGHTENED INTEREST

Anheuser-Busch, brewer of Budweiser, is also a major user of aluminum in its canned products. Its Metal Container Corporation produces more than 20 billion cans and 20 billion lids annually at its 11 can and lid manufacturing facilities. It supplies about 60% of Anheuser-Busch's container and lid requirements and is a significant supplier to the US soft-drink container market.

Its commitment to recycling has turned it into one of the world's largest recyclers of aluminum and this activity into a profitable business.

"Anheuser-Busch Recycling Corporation provides a positive alternative to mandatory deposits and helps reduce container costs. As the world's largest recycler of aluminum beverage containers, Anheuser-Busch Recycling Corporation recycles the equivalent of about 125 percent of the beer cans Anheuser-Busch ships domestically."[1]

So the self-enlightened company can engage in social value type debates and make an active contribution. Subsequently it can and should look to situate profitable activity within this debate context. Making a profit does not invalidate the sincerity of the engagement. But not following concrete deeds with a worthy policy statement surely will. This leads us on to the first major new activity within reputation management – that of corporate branding. Product branding really grew up in the 20th century – beginning as a way of differentiating between commodity suppliers such as sugar, coffee and grain. By the end of the century branding was a sophisticated and all-pervasive enterprise, becoming – as Y&R, the advertising agency, was to claim – somehow a surrogate for lost religious belief.

This would presumably turn the marketers into the new high priests of contemporary civilization. Presumably, they will be equally well placed as their predecessors to mystify the populations at large.

While we have grown more comfortable with and used to the role of product brands in our society, the notion that a company has its own brand which extends beyond mere familiarity is quite new. In other words, we have always made judgments about companies based on what we know or think we know about them. But the idea that this "reputation" could be turned into a dynamic enterprise by corporations for business value is much more recent.

As John Graham, the charismatic chairman and chief executive officer of Fleishman-Hillard, the largest PR firm in the US said: "there are meetings going on right across the country [US] about corporate branding, what it means and how it can be achieved."

Within PR/communication/perception management agencies, corporate branding management represents a new discipline and, of course, new lucrative lines of business. The latter will be most welcome, as e-economy consulting revenues are crashing and burning.

INTRODUCING CORPORATE BRANDING

The business need has sprouted from a vague but growing appreciation in the business community that the "value" of a company is more than just the numbers on an asset sheet or indeed the "goodwill" represented by the brand equity of its products.

Other "intangible" (or softer) factors come into play – including the profile/persona of the CEO and the interplay between a company and a range of audiences, such as local communities, financial analysts, NGOs, employees, suppliers, day-traders, and so on. The realization by many senior business managers is that these intangibles can be (and indeed need to be) managed. The health of the business (and their careers) depends on it.

Outside commentators often view the ability to manage these soft and difficult issues as an overall sign of strength. Examples of good corporate branding or (re-branding) would include BP, which, as we have discussed, along with being the most profitable oil company in the world has won over many environmentalists with its controversial **B**eyond **P**etroleum (BP) stance.

There are also good financial gains to be made in this area. The corporate re-branding of Andersen Consulting to Accenture ran up a £20 mn bill. 3iI (the venture capitalist group), which now rejoices under the strap-line "The World is Yours", has also committed a seven-figure sum to its re-branding exercise.

WHAT'S NEW ABOUT CORPORATE BRANDING?

The first and perhaps most important question about corporate branding is what makes it different from product branding – aside, of course, from the fact that the product is now a corporation rather than a can of soft drink. Encouragingly for PR or communication businesses, the answer lies in the type of practitioner. In product branding, advertising usually led the way – both in terms of budget allocation and in terms of overall importance within the marketing mix. Corporate branding covers a more complex set of audiences – stakeholders direct and indirect (see Chapter 2 "What is Reputation Management?"). You cannot buy your way into their hearts and minds by putting a well-designed advertisement into a relevant publication.

While successful product branding usually revolves around simple well-honed messages – such as Nike is cool and ballsy ("Just Do It") or McDonald's is a family experience (the character Ronald McDonald) – corporate branding will inevitably be pushing out more complex messages.

In summary, corporate branding activity will involve more complex messages towards more diffuse sets of audiences than product advertising. Of course there are also (as we have seen) indirect sets of audiences which need to be influenced, for example regulators who legislate on your business. A recent high-profile activity at establishing a new corporate brand happened in the launch of Accenture (formerly Andersen Consulting).

CORPORATE RE-BRANDING: FROM ANDERSEN CONSULTING TO ACCENTURE

"The name 'Accenture' is, after all, an empty vessel."

Accenture.com

We know what they say about empty vessels making most noise. And there has been a lot of noise surrounding the launch of the new brand – following the shotgun divorce between the accounting and management consulting arms of Andersen.

In some ways, launching the new brand at the beginning of the new millennium could be seen as serendipitous. Accenture sees itself as both a symbol and a catalyst of the new economy – and there is something very "old economy" about accounting firms. As the end of one Monty Python show put it:

"if you have any ideas, send them in on a postcard to the following address . . . If you don't have any ideas, try accounting . . ."

Albeit firmly positioning themselves as "virtual" ambassadors from the virtual world, there were some very "terrestrial" tasks to be achieved – with 50 teams being designated to implement changes throughout 137 offices worldwide. It involved activities from communicating with 20,000 client executives and hundreds of thousands of recruitment candidates to printing 6.5 million new business cards.

The re-branding exercise, costing tens of millions of hard-earned (client) dollars has resulted in "approximately 1,000 milestones to track during the next few months," according to Thomas Pollan, partner at Process, Financial Services.

CORPORATE SOCIAL RESPONSIBILITY

An off-shoot of corporate branding is what is being termed *corporate social responsibility (CSR)* – loosely how a corporation's reputation plays out in environmental terms

CSR is defined as the holistic response and contribution, going beyond basic legal requirements and based on enlightened self-interest, of individual businesses to the broader, global transition to sustainable development – broadly speaking, how the corporate brand plays out in environmental terms

CSR stands in a long tradition of corporate ethics, which can trace its modern roots to the work of the Cadbury family (chocolate manufacturers) in Bournville in the UK. Late twentieth-century examples include Ben & Jerry's and Body Shop International. In both the nineteenth and twentieth centuries, a few leading companies have raised standards across the business community.

Corporate reputation increasingly depends on being seen to be in step with societal expectations, and in a radically transparent world the penalties for falling short can be severe. The guiding principle behind companies that practice CSR is that it is not enough simply to give away a slice of profits to solve social and environmental problems. Instead, business must be conducted in ways that minimize social and environmental problems in the first place, thus spreading the benefits of globalization. Indeed, CSR is the private sector's contribution to the broader, global effort towards sustainable development – a movement which in turn flows from widespread public concern about the future. In this way CSR could be seen as inoculating the business against being targeted by the anti-globalization protesters.

CSR covers every impact that a company has: its own workforce, local communities, supplier employees at home and abroad, and the environment. Environmental concerns have dominated the debate in recent decades, partly because these impacts are easier to measure than "fair wages" or "community capacity building." Large environmental challenges remain (climate change, biodiversity conservation, elimination of toxics, and so on), but with the advent of the Internet and 24-hour media, combined with the restructuring caused by intense global competition, attention is also switching to how employees are treated wherever they sit in the supply chain.

ALL WORDS AND NO ACTION?

Earlier, we looked at the dangers inherent in not following up nice user-friendly aspirations with concrete actions. A study conducted for the Australian Institute of Company Directors, covering 98 leading public and private companies, shows that "while there is clearly a willingness to engage in corporate citizenship, much of it is aspirational and not actually embedded in company policy or practice."

According to researcher professor Birch: "most firms see corporate citizenship as short-term community involvement, like sponsoring the arts, sport or charities."[2]

Professor Birch believes the key difficulty facing business is how to demonstrate that commitment through actions makes business sense that can be argued through a business case and that can be evaluated and measured.

One such case in point of action following words on a matter of strong social environmental impact concerns Unilever – owner of Best Foods, Ben & Jerry's and Lipton.

CSR in action: Marine Stewardship Council (MSC)

The MSC was founded in 1997 as a result of the effects on the ecosystem of over-fishing and the potential environmental catastrophe if something was not done. The organization was founded by Unilever, one of the world's largest buyers of frozen fish, and the World Wide Fund for Nature (WWF), the international conservation organization. While the two organizations had different motivations they had the same goal. Unilever, which owns many valuable seafood brands including Gorton's, Findus, Bird's Eye, and Iglo, realized that the commercial future of these companies was jeopardized if efforts were not stepped up to reverse the threat posed by over-fishing.

During 1997 and 1998, the MSC also moved towards its crucial independence from Unilever and WWF, broadening its base of support and seeking new funding. By 1999, it had become fully independent of its two founders and was able to expand its staff and increase its profile as a serious participant in the marine conservation debate. The first fisheries came forward for certification and supermarkets, especially in the US and UK, increased their activities to prepare for the arrival of labeled products.

In November 2000, Unilever launched its first product carrying the Marine Stewardship Council logo, which informs consumers that the brand has been sourced from "sustainable" fisheries. The salmon product, fillets in a marinated sauce, is being sold under the Iglo brand by Pierrot-Lusso in Switzerland, and comes from a salmon fishery in Alaska.

STATE OF THE ART: THE AGENCY BUSINESS

Viral marketing

Many PR/communications agencies have set up a department/service offering to cater for new media clients. With the dot.com boom (and then bust), many have refocused on the digital/new media aspect of their old economy clients ("bricks & clicks"). For the most part this amounts to plain vanilla PR with some "E"s prefixed here and there.

The paradigm has shifted? On closer examination of PR agencies' businesses, it becomes clear that not many have substantively reorganized themselves (operationally) to cater for the shifted paradigm which the digital economy (in their own view) represented. A case of "do as I say, not as I do." The typical PR agency (on the whole) conducts its business the same way today as it would have done in 1990.

Hi-tech agencies (those with organizations such as Microsoft or Dell as clients) have done very well. Hi-tech agencies have grown 20% or more annually since the mid-1990s. But it must be realized that at the core of this activity is solid (old-fashioned) trade media relations. At the end of the day this is what "shifts boxes."

Viral marketing/buzz marketing,[3] which (one would imagine) is tailor-made[4] for a PR new media business, is just not being done competently. If there were ever a topic which would allow the PR industry to establish primacy over advertising and management consulting, it is this offering. However, as indicated earlier, it needs a mature and multiskilled approach for credible delivery.

Financial PR

This sector is where the greatest margin can be made and where a value sell seems easiest – priced on success rather than on billable hours. Financial PR is still seen as a very networked part of the business, i.e. relying heavily on contacts.

Trends

» Calendar (commodity) financial work – (quarterly results, etc.) will migrate in-house.
» New media will have an impact (e.g. streamed video content on Websites) with investment banks putting recordings of their analyst briefings on Websites as a move toward greater transparency. Would see good uptake by day-traders and investment clubs.
» Continued good margin and volume business in M&As.

Consumer

This is where we find good volume business but very tight margins. Normally working to a marketing/brand director, budgets are much less "elastic" than, say, on an M&A project. The large agencies are constantly being pushed by young upstarts with trendy names (Cake, Slice, Red, Shine). The upstarts cite creativity as their core value with the implication being that it is hard for the bigger agencies to sustain creative work or retain truly creative people. The upstarts can punch more than their weight.

Traditionally and popularly (i.e. as depicted in *Absolutely Fabulous*) associated with the fashion and travel industries, the perception of PR as a glamorous career was born here.

Latterly, though, fashion and travel budgets have remained very small or fragmented and many consumer agencies and divisions are relying on the TMT and food and drink sectors for growth.

Trends

» *Holistic and experiential marketing*. Cutting through the jargon, this appears to amount to getting the consumer to interact with the brand more directly. For example, getting Tiger Woods into Hyde Park supported by his sponsors or staging a club night sponsored by and themed with Lynx body spray.

» *Companies owning the channels*, e.g. *Marie Claire* being owned by L'Oreal.

KEY LEARNING POINTS

» Reputation management – particularly when applied to corporations – is still a young discipline.
» It is becoming apparent that if corporations do not engage in environmental or social debates sincerely (i.e. with a view to making a real difference) they will get exposed as self-interested and short-termist.
» It is possible to have enlightened self-interest – i.e. realize your business objective through sincere engagement with an issue.
» Building in extra values to your reputation is currently being termed "corporate branding" and it has many similarities with the traditional product brand – in that extra values are being assigned to the entity. An off-shoot of corporate branding is what is being termed "corporate social responsibility" (CSR) – loosely how a corporation's reputation plays out in environmental terms.

NOTES

1 www.anheuser-busch.com
2 www.companydirectors.com.au/index.html
3 See Gladwell, M. (2000) *The Tipping Point: How Little Things Can Make a Big Difference*. Little Brown, New York.
4 The Internet loves rumor, the unofficial, and the sharing of personal values with the many. Look at the success of The Drudge Report or ain't-it-cool-news.com. Of course, viral marketing pre-dates the popular use of the Internet – but the Net is a natural home.

In Practice

This chapter takes a look at how corporate reputation has fared in differing circumstances and in differing parts of the world. Initially we take an extensive look at how Shell, one of the world's largest companies, was brought to its knees by Greenpeace over the dumping of the *Brent Spar* oil rig: *Reputation Lost*. We then look at how reputation can be regained through looking at how a chemical manufacturer based in Venezuela – Bitor – rebuilt its tarnished reputation through reputation building activity: *Reputation Regained*. Finally we take a look at how the corporate giant Unilever looked to establish itself in China: *Building Reputation*.

REPUTATION LOST. *BRENT SPAR* : THE BATTLE BETWEEN ROYAL DUTCH/SHELL AND GREENPEACE

A year after the conflict over the dumping at sea of the oil platform the *Brent Spar*, Shell declared that:

> "*Brent Spar* is no longer just a North Sea installation, but a unique and defining event. The challenge now is to ensure that it defines a new stage in the regulation of business which employs the hearts as well as minds."[1]

But what exactly was being defined? What had happened to one of the world's biggest corporations that it was conceding that an oil rig – a simple tool of the oil trade – was being used as a tool to change the regulatory conditions of its business?

The center of balance had moved away from the business – it was losing control over how it wished to conduct its own affairs – and it had done nothing illegal! The way it wished to conduct its business was partly being handed over to those who knew little and cared even less about the oil trade.

Having taken the *Brent Spar* out of operation, Shell, the world's biggest petrol retailer, surveyed a number of options to dispose of the facility before deciding to dump it in the north Atlantic. The disposal plan was approved in February 1995 by the UK government, which also informed the other EC member states. However, on June 20, 1995 – just four months later, Shell postponed its plans to dispose of the *Spar* at high financial and corporate cost to itself and embarked on a wide public consultation process.

ROYAL DUTCH/SHELL

Royal Dutch/Shell operates throughout the world, in more than 130 countries and with more than 100,000 staff. It has a global network of more than 46,000 petrol stations – Shell companies serve approximately 20 million fuel customers every day.

GREENPEACE

Greenpeace is a global environmental organization campaigning, on subjects such as the protection of oceans and ancient forests, the phasing-out of fossil fuels, and the promotion of renewable energies in order to stop climate change. The Greenpeace organization consists of Greenpeace International (Stichting Greenpeace Council) in Amsterdam and Greenpeace offices around the world. Greenpeace currently has a presence in 41 countries. Greenpeace is committed to the principles of non-violence, political independence, and internationalism.

So what happened?

First let us look at the history behind Greenpeace's attempt to get into the business of lobbying against oil companies. Although Greenpeace had attempted to protect US coastal waters by campaigning against oil drilling and prospecting in ecologically sensitive areas as far back as 1983, it was not until 1989 – after the *Exxon Valdez* sank in Prince William Sound, Alaska, spilling 40 millions gallons of oil – that Greenpeace formally began to campaign on oil.

Greenpeace acknowledged the difficulty of such a campaign because of the western world's obvious dependence on oil.

This required a more complex campaign message to be pushed out – as distinct from bashing baby seals with clubs, for example, which was always a simple and effective fund-raising platform.

Greenpeace set itself two targets on the oil campaign: first to highlight "dubious" industry practices, and second to attempt to educate the public on alternative sources of energy.

A series of oil disasters in the next few years began to give Greenpeace opportunities to push out their message: pollution linked to oil wells in Siberia in 1991; in 1992, the *Haven* caught fire and sank in the Mediterranean; in 1993 the *Braer* oil tanker ran aground off the coast of the Shetland Isles, releasing twice as much oil as the *Valdez*.

Of course, the difficulty for Greenpeace lay in the fact that it could not actually try to block the normal progress of oil tankers around the world – the result of that would have been to lose some public support.

Additionally, when an oil disaster struck, what role could Greenpeace usefully play, aside from saying "we told you so?" It could perhaps help in the clean-up activities, as when it lent the rescue services an oil boom when the oil tanker *Rose Bay* ran aground off the coast of Devon in the UK. No sexy headlines there.

The opportunity

Halfway through 1994, Greenpeace became aware that the UK government was reviewing plans for disposing of obsolete rigs at sea. Greenpeace was later to claim that its only interest at the time was to present its arguments against sea dumping. Regardless of whether that was ever really the case, in December of 1994 the UK government's Department of Trade and Industry wrote a key report. This was in favor of the disposal at sea of the *Brent Spar*. The path was laid open for what was to become one of Greenpeace's most successful campaigns.

Part of Shell's problems throughout the affair was summed up by Cor Herkstroter, chairman of Royal Dutch (the Dutch half of Royal Dutch/Shell) as "technical arrogance." Which is to say, once the technical aspects of the problems had been investigated and a decision taken, an arrogance and lack of sensitivity to other side of the issue would set in. As far as Shell was concerned, it had done its bit by commissioning the leading offshore engineering and marine contracting firm McDermott. It had reached the conclusion that the sea disposal of the *Brent Spar* constituted "deep sea disposal."

This was then proposed to the UK government, which then was happy to issue a license. Anything else, as far as Shell was concerned, was secondary.

The technical bases had been covered and there was little need for the organization to concern itself with a debate on the subject. Moreover, it considered (mistakenly) that because it had the law on its side it could just force the issue through.

The bay of rigs

The battle on the *Brent Spar*, which in Shell's own words was to become a "unique and defining event," was planned by Greenpeace in March 1995. Their game plan: to place a number of activists on board. Greenpeace knew that Shell had only a limited amount of time to dispose of the rig before the inclement weather of the North Sea began to set in after the short summer. Their mission: to delay the disposal operation as long as possible in the hope that the "window of opportunity would pass."

On April 30, four activists clambered on board and raised the banner – "Save the North Sea." The victim had been identified and this time Greenpeace was on hand in a visible and eminently communicable fashion. The message to their membership and beyond: this time we can stop an oil disaster before it actually happens.

Greenpeace's media apparatus captured these "defining" moments and broadcast them to news agencies across the world.

Greenpeace was later to recall that the atmosphere once aboard was eerie.

"In the office areas there was still a great deal of information in the cupboards and personal effects such as postcards – it's as if everybody left in a hurry. The movement of the sea made loose doors creak open and shut, adding to the illusion of the ghost ship."[2]

After two weeks of occupation, the first sign of erosion in Shell's comfort zone had occurred. Up until this point, the fact that the UK government had made the grant of a license had at least battened down the argument from a regulatory perspective. However, on May 12, 1995, the Danish government criticized the granting of the license. The regulatory sweater which was keeping Shell warm was beginning to unravel. Later that day Shell served a legal eviction order on the protesters.

Shell attained an interdict from a Scottish court stopping the re-supply of the *Spar*. An attempt by Greenpeace to relieve the protesters on board on Day 17 of the occupation was aggressively hampered by Shell.

Further unraveling of the regulatory position continued when Germany, Belgium, and Iceland joined the protest against the granting of the license. The UK government stood firm. Things then began to move very quickly indeed.

COUNTDOWN TO CORPORATE FAILURE

May 18, 1995: Shell gets an eviction order naming Jon Castle – the Greenpeace leader on the *Spar*.

May 24: An oil rig support vessel, several times the size of the *Brent Spar*, arrives on the scene and police and security finally manage to remove the protesters.

June 7: Greenpeace manages to place more protesters on the rig and hang a banner – "Save our Seas." They are driven off by water cannon.

June 9: Ireland joins the protest against the granting of a license.
Over the following Ten days:

» Mounting pressure on the UK government from other country representatives continues. Again, the UK government stands resolute.
» Media attention on the issue escalates.
» Greenpeace organizes protests at Shell offices across Europe.
» There are public protests at Shell service stations across Europe including gun-fire aimed at a service station in Germany.

June 20: Greenpeace manages to place two activists on board the *Spar*. Shell backs down on the plans to sink the *Spar*. The *Brent Spar* is dragged away by the defeated tugs and a huge rainbow (Greenpeace's logo) is visible in the victorious sky.

An unexpected turn: Greenpeace apologizes

In September, Greenpeace apologized to Shell because it had actually miscalculated (and overestimated) the amount of toxic waste which was on board the *Spar*. The amount of toxic waste on board had played a key part in Greenpeace's argument that the *Spar* should not be dumped at sea. In a release and public letter of apology, Peter Melchett, executive director of Greenpeace stated:

"The argument was about whether it was right to dump industrial waste of any sort in the deep oceans, whether dumping the *Brent Spar* would be a precedent for dumping other oil installations, and indeed other wastes in the oceans, and, fundamentally, over whether we should dump wastes into any part of the environment, as opposed to reducing waste, and recycling, treating, or containing harmful materials.

"Our view remains that the division between us on the *Brent Spar* depends on how deeply we value our environment, and what damage and precedents we find unacceptable. As information about our sampling on the *Brent Spar* was made available to the press, I am making this letter similarly available, and I would be grateful if you could convey my apologies to your colleagues on the Board of Shell UK."

Later that month, the two sides moved closer together when Greenpeace publicly welcomed 21 out of the 29 proposals being considered by Shell for the disposal of the *Spar*. Greenpeace comments:

"The signs are that Shell is now following the logic of environmental responsibility and public opinion."[3]

The net result

Shell's power over one of its own vessels, with a full and legal disposal license, had been taken away from it by a group of protesters acting illegally and with inaccurate data about how much waste was on board in the first place.

Although Shell's share price seemed to have been largely unaffected by the saga, it does admit that the debacle over the *Spar* may have cost them "a great deal" in the short term. There are a host of oil rigs waited to be disposed of, but the rest of the oil industry still appears afraid to go down the same road as Shell – each wants the other to go first; as Greenpeace smugly remarked "there is a race to come second."

Shell's reputation in the longer term was also severely hit by its technical arrogance. It became a symbol of what was wrong about the oil industry and indeed with big business in general. What had started out as the dismantling at sea of an oil rig turned out to be the dismantling of a corporate reputation which has still yet to recover fully.

KEY LEARNING POINTS REGARDING GREENPEACE TACTICS

» Greenpeace establishes the position closest to the environment (as an absolute value).

» Greenpeace sets out its stall – and establishes a distance between itself and Shell.

» This necessarily places Shell further away from the environment.

» This in turn makes it a lot easier to expose Shell's motives (profit/greed) and not Greenpeace's. Why not the latter? Simply because of its proximity to the environment.

» From the beginning of the engagement Greenpeace is at an advantage, although it seems to be the more helpless.

» Shell allowed Greenpeace to set the agenda and thereby was always one move behind. For example, it was only when Shell's public policy position began to crumble, (May 12: Danish government criticizes the granting of a license) that it served the eviction notice on the protesters. It is probably fair to assume that Shell had been seeking to hold off as long as possible from tactically engaging with Greenpeace on the *Spar*. Scuffles at sea with corporations or law enforcement representatives is the sea activist's forte – so that the latter move would have been to the delight of Greenpeace.

» Tactics which Shell might have considered:

1 expose Greenpeace's care for the environment as not disinterested: the environment is only a pawn in its quest of power;

2 achieve a higher ground in the public and public policy eye on the environment – thereby corrupting Greenpeace's privileged position; and

3 seek to substitute a different absolute value in place of the environment – the public's need for fuel to keep civilization on track, for example.

None of this would have been easy to do, and without the benefit of hindsight perhaps it would have been difficult to make the argument internally to allocate the resources needed to achieve these ends.

REPUTATION REGAINED: BITOR, VENEZUELA[4]

BITOR

Bitor is a wholly owned subsidiary of the Venezuelan state oil company, PDVSA. Bitor's sole product is a fuel oil called Orimulsion, which was developed in conjunction with BP in the 1980s (BP has since sold back its intellectual property rights in Orimulsion to Bitor).

Orimulsion is an emulsion of 70% bitumen and 30% water, kept stable by a chemical surfactant. Orimulsion offers a competitive alternative to coal for burning in power stations. Venezuela has vast and largely untapped reserves of the bitumen needed to create the fuel oil.

However, Orimulsion contains more sulfur than most coal and when, in 1995, a generating company applied to burn it in Pembrokeshire, West Wales, without any flue-gas desulfurization technology, it attracted a predictably fierce campaign of opposition, led with some style by Friends of the Earth. The high sulfur content and the alleged "gender bending" properties of the surfactant were the main concerns and Orimulsion quickly acquired the tag of "the world's filthiest fuel."

Then, in an unfortunate coincidence, while the planning permission to burn Orimulsion in Pembrokeshire was still in the balance, an oil tanker named *Sea Empress* ran aground in Milford Haven, just a few miles from the fuel oil terminal where Orimulsion would have been imported. The resulting oil slick from the *Sea Empress* attracted widespread media coverage, complete with shots of dead marine life smothered in black crude, and this spelled the end of the planning application. It was also, as it happens, the end of the power station, which had been depending on Orimulsion for a new lease of life. It closed soon afterwards, with the loss of hundreds of jobs in already economically fragile local Welsh communities.

Just when it seemed that things could not get much worse for Bitor, a second application to burn Orimulsion, this time at a power station in Florida, was also defeated. This setback was largely the result of a concerted local campaign by the Sierra Club. Yet, all the time Orimulsion was under attack in the UK and the US, Orimulsion was being successfully burnt in Canada, Japan, and Denmark, under strict environmental conditions, and was demonstrating some real advantages over coal – such as producing 15% less carbon dioxide and 99% less ash, all of which is recyclable. In a world where both demand for energy and concern about the environment are rising quickly, Orimulsion is a vital component of the global energy mix and a useful transition fuel as the market for renewable power sources slowly matures.

In both Pembroke and Florida, the generating companies had done all the talking, leaving Bitor itself without a voice. After its negative experiences there, Bitor decided to take control of its own destiny. It began an initially cautious round of discussions with some of its most prominent critics, seeking not to promote Orimulsion, or even to change opinions about the merits of the product, but simply to understand the expectations of key stakeholders. It listened, it learned a lot about what their critics thought would constitute responsible behavior, and it decided to act.

Bitor did three things as a direct result of its consultations. First, it made a public commitment that it would sign contracts to supply Orimulsion only to those power stations fitted with proper flue-gas desulfurization equipment in line with World Bank environmental guidelines, even though this would cost Bitor some contracts. Second, it changed the surfactant used in Orimulsion, even though the scientific view was that there was nothing wrong with the original one. The new surfactant is alcohol-based and totally environmentally benign. Third, it instructed its distributors that Orimulsion should only be shipped in double-hulled tankers, thus minimizing the risk of any spillages in the event of marine accidents (the UK government report into the *Sea Empress* disaster concluded that had the tanker been double-hulled, it is highly unlikely that any oil would have escaped when it ran aground in Milford Haven).

These changes to the way in which Bitor conducts its business did not resolve all the issues, and discussions are still going on with Friends of the Earth about the possible health implications of ultra-fine particles in the exhaust gases, but these tangible policy changes did achieve a huge amount for Bitor's reputation. When it next found itself face to face with the assembled NGO community, at an International Finance Corporation workshop in Washington DC, it received public praise from Friends of the Earth for its "responsible attitude." One potential outcome of this IFC workshop was that World Bank funding for any power supply projects that involved burning Orimulsion could have been blocked on environmental grounds, effectively excluding Bitor from dozens of commercial opportunities in the developing world, where demand for energy is growing fastest. Instead, following the constructive discussions among the stakeholders, the IFC agreed to treat Orimulsion just like any other fossil fuel and to treat funding applications that involve Orimulsion on their merits on a case-by-case basis. This is precisely the outcome that Bitor wanted.

Now, a couple of years further on, three highly regarded and independent-minded environmentalists are working with the company, as an independent environment and development advisory committee, to improve further the company's policies and practices and to help the company engage with local stakeholders when new commercial opportunities arise. None of this, of course, will have changed Friends of the Earth's view that burning black fossil fuels is a thoroughly bad thing to be doing in the face of the global warming threat, and it doesn't even mean that future applications to burn Orimulsion will necessarily be approved, but Bitor's reputation is certainly very much better than it was before the company set out to understand the expectations of some of its key stakeholders.

For instance, Bitor's next planning application after the setbacks in Pembrokeshire and Florida was a proposal to burn Orimulsion in a power station in Northern Ireland. Friends of the Earth took an interest in the application but did not condemn it and changed the references to Orimulsion on their much-visited Website from "the world's filthiest fuel" to "a potentially polluting fuel." Bitor has helped to convene a local stakeholder forum to discuss the concerns of residents and final planning permission is expected to be a formality.

KEY LEARNING POINTS

» The best way of establishing and understanding expectations is to hold face-to-face meetings and to develop constructive working relationships with current and potential critics.

» This process needs to be properly managed, and kept as informal as possible, and there is always a need for an "honest broker" to make the initial introductions and to facilitate the dialogue.

» The process of dialogue need not be complicated or surrounded in jargon.

» Where communications are concerned, stakeholders can be divided into specialists (namely people who are comfortable with the language of sustainability, such as institutional investors, NGOs, suppliers, and corporate customers) and non-specialists (namely employees, consumers, and local communities).

» The specialists are best talked to individually; and the non-specialists in groups. Either way it is a time-consuming process but it does deliver high-quality information and in some cases make or break the company under scrutiny.

BUILDING REPUTATION: UNILEVER IN CHINA

China, at first glance, offers the internal business both a dazzling and a complex opportunity: a population of 1.2 billion representing 56 nationalities but with few natural resources. Politically closed but economically open.

In 2000, China's GDP was US$1trn with US$42bn of foreign investment. It is still a very regulated marketplace boasting no less than 11 million government officials. It has just under 1,000 TV stations and over 2,000 newspapers – all of which are government run.

With the recent opening up of China to international trade, the consumer is faced with a new and dazzling array of products on the supermarket shelf. For the brand builder, this race for share of mind can be particularly tough.

Packaging and price points are all fairly similar. Packaging suppliers for some of Unilever's brands are also suppliers to local brands. With such "equivalence" going on, the question in the consumer's mind is "what criteria should they use to differentiate?" How can they determine if a product is backed up by proper R&D, safety, and quality standards?

While consumers in many countries do not know or care which multinational giant is behind a particular brand (Unilever, P&G, Nestlé), consumers in China most certainly do. This immediately puts the relations between the corporation and the consumer brand into the frame. A good corporate citizen in China will add value to the actual product brand.

Twenty years ago, household products from international firms had a certain cachet. That is no longer the case – although there are certainly higher expectations of international businesses within the country. There is an implicit acknowledgment by Chinese consumers – particularly the more sophisticated ones – that China is a lucrative market, and international businesses need to work hard to deserve their attention.

UNILEVER

Unilever, the foods and detergents giant, turned over $45bn in 2000, employing more than 246,000. In the US it owns Best Foods, SlimFast and Ben & Jerry's as well as Lipton. Other well-known brands internationally include: Dove, Magnum, Omo, and Cif. Unilever formally entered the Chinese market in 1986 and has 17 brands there in three key business groups – Home & Personal Care, Food, and Ice Cream.

Good relations with government – locally and nationally – are key to business success

Because of the regulated nature of the marketplace in China, businesses need licenses to operate in many areas. This places a huge emphasis on the public affairs activity of international businesses. One of the most successful initiatives in which Unilever engaged to build reputation with key stakeholders concerned the complex subject of phosphates and water.

Detergents contain phosphates that might be washed directly into rivers. Eutrophication is the natural process by which waters (lakes, rivers, etc.) become enriched with nutrients, typically nitrogen and phosphorus. However, increased concentrations of nutrients encourage the growth of organisms such as algae. Their demand for oxygen, especially at night, can outstrip the supply, which can harm aquatic life. The process can make the water taste unpleasant and may, in some cases, endanger life. Fish, for example, can be asphyxiated or poisoned by toxins released by some algae. Some argue, therefore, that detergents can lead to dead fish.

As a major manufacturer of detergents Unilever has become very knowledgable about the impact of phosphates on the environment.

The issue of eutrophication is also high on the priority list of the Chinese Environmental Protection Agency (EPA). Water shortages and pollution are major concerns, with almost all water masses polluted and 300 cities experiencing water shortages. At a consumer level, 63% of urban residents name the environment as the No.1 issue of concern.

Unilever organized an education tour for the EPA to its historic facilities at Port Sunlight just across the river Mersey from Liverpool, in the UK. The tour, which also took in the water treatment facilities, focused on imparting much of what Unilever has learned about the whole issue. This simple educational tour had a big impact on the EPA and is typical of what genuine knowledge sharing can do to enhance fundamental relationships.

KEY LEARNING POINTS

» Look for win–win situations – where natural concerns of the consumers can be met with assets groups of the business; here environmental awareness among the stakeholders and the public at large is matched with Unilever's strong environmental heritage and credentials.

» Look to harness increased corporate reputation to sales growth – in China the two are linked in the consumer's mind.

» Look to the long term – building reputation takes time.

» Have measurable results. Do not engage in "responsible" projects unless they have a link to the business activity and thrust.

NOTES

1 www.shell.com
2 www.greenpeace.org
3 www.greenpeace.org
4 Material submitted by Richard Aylard and Nick Bent, Directors, Burson-Marsteller CSR Unit, London. See www.bm.com/insights/corpresp.html and www.orimulsionfuel.com

Key Concepts and Thinkers

This chapter presents an A–Z glossary of reputation management which includes key concepts and practitioners.

A GLOSSARY OF REPUTATION MANAGEMENT

Audience – Audiences must be identified and distinct messages channeled towards them. Audiences can be broken down into the following sections:

» public affairs audiences – government and politicians;
» media – local, national, and international;
» business partners – franchisees, distributors, marketing partners, and suppliers;
» financial audiences – analysts, investors, shareholders;
» internal audiences – employees, trade unions;
» potential recruits; and
» customers.

Brand (corporate) – The business need for corporate branding has sprouted from a vague but growing appreciation in the business community that the "value" of a company is more than just the numbers on an asset sheet or indeed the "goodwill" represented by the brand equity of its products.

Other "intangible" (or softer) factors come into play – including the profile/persona of the CEO; the interplay between a company and a range of audiences, such as local communities, financial analysts, NGOs, employees, suppliers, day-traders, and so on. The realization by many senior business managers is that these intangibles can be (and indeed need to be) managed. The health of the business (and their careers) depends on it.

Outside commentators often view the ability to manage these soft and difficult issues as an overall sign of strength. Examples of good corporate branding or (re-branding) would include BP.

Communication – What we have to do in order to move those audiences closer to our business objective.

Corporate social responsibility (CSR) – An offshoot of corporate branding, CSR refers loosely to how a corporation's reputation plays out in environmental terms. CSR is defined as the holistic response and contribution, going beyond basic legal requirements and based on enlightened self-interest of individual businesses to the broader, global transition to sustainable development.

Credibility – If communication is an information transaction between parties then credibility is the currency. You must safeguard the value of the currency else the words may be perfect but have little impact – due to poor credibility.

Daniel Defoe – Writer of *Moll Flanders* and *Robinson Crusoe*: both books give us key insights into how reputation actually operates: An early learning point of the work *Moll Flanders* is that "reputation" is a social or external convention. It is not based on what we ourselves think it is (or even ought to be). It is based on external perceptions and values. Like Moll, a corporation can seek to rise above the realities of its origin, heritage, or baggage. But also (like Moll) it needs to have a level of honesty and self-awareness of its current standing in order to be able to do so successfully. Robinson Crusoe, when firmly planted on the island, did not need to worry about managing his reputation because he went to a place where his status and conventions had no currency. The island was an environment in which Robinson had to learn a new pecking order – and he was only nominally its master. More importantly, as he was alone on the island, the concept of reputation and hence its management was redundant. Again, "reputation" is a social or relational convention. Robinson did not have a "society" on the island with whom he could relate. It was only when "Man Friday" came on the scene that he was presented with the opportunity of both relating to another human being, and establishing a master–servant rapport. At this juncture in the book the issue of "how" he was perceived by Man Friday (and hence his reputation) enters the equation.

Electronic age – This poses opportunities as well as threats when it comes to the management of one's corporate reputation. The digital age provides the manager with very sophisticated tools for disseminating information to a whole range of internal and external stakeholders. But the "brave new world" also opens up the company so that the distinction between outside and inside is actually blurred. When it comes to management of reputation this perhaps is one of the greatest challenges posed by the age of e-business. The Internet culture shares information, and perpetuates truths and rumors. In fact it blurs the difference and treats them with equal respect. So what does this mean for business people? If you're a big-time polluter or treat people – employees, customers, shareholders – badly, then you're in for a rough ride. If not, then the important lesson is about how you get things done.

Fleishman-Hillard – Largest PR firm in the US, with its headquarters in St. Louis. It has built a very successful international business under John Graham; it is now part of the Omnicom Group. Fleishman-Hillard has also maintained some long-standing business relationships, such as that with Anheuser-Busch – the world's largest brewer.

Globalization – One of the biggest drivers of globalization will be technology, according to the National Intelligence Council.

> "The integration of information technology, biotechnology, materials sciences, and nanotechnology will generate a dramatic increase in innovation.
>
> "The time between the discovery and the application of scientific advances will continue to shorten. Developments in the laboratory will reach commercial production at ever faster rates, leading to increased investments."

Business can no longer rely on governments to educate on these innovations – they will be doing their best merely to regulate. Similarly, business cannot leave the stage clear to NGOs to champion the cause of the consumer – this would merely result in a climate of fear and suspicion. The commercial value of speed to market will see a growth in the number of "public permission" hurdles to be encountered by the technology innovators.

Human resources – The most valuable asset in the business. People buy people. See also "Internal."

Internal – Corporate reputation management begins at home. There is little point in pushing out warm words to the external market and behaving differently to employees. If a company wishes to engage in frank open dialogue with stakeholders it must first exemplify that type of behavior within. Managers should remember that the whole organization (salespeople, call-center operators, reception, security, accounts, engineers, and so on) communicates values every day to a vast network of audiences.

In the old economy, there were only a few points of contact regulating information between the inside and outside of the organization, such as media spokespeople, analyst liaison officers, and personnel managers. In fact, the neat distinction between what lies inside and outside an organization is now becoming more difficult to make.

The proliferation of the Internet, e-mail, and supplier portals makes it easier for the outside world to interact continuously with people on the inside.

Journalist – The 21st-century journalist has come under increasing pressure. You see everywhere examples of the proliferation and the fragmentation of the media industry – be it 200 digital channels or the Internet channels – but the advertising budgets which support all of this is relatively finite. This means that journalists are asked to cover more and more stories, being disseminated through a wider variety of media, all with the same or even diminishing resources. The Internet is also forcing the time pressure on journalists. The famous Monica Lewinsky story was known to "Newsweek" well before the Internet news site The Drudge Report first published. But because the Internet published first it forced the hand of the established terrestrial media to publish. The competing players of the media industry like to be first with the story in an effort to gain and retain the interest of the audience.

What this means for you before you engage with the journalist is that there is a both an opportunity as well as a threat. It is an opportunity because the journalist typically knows a hell of a little about a hell of a lot – they may cover financial services one day and the technology sector the next. Their knowledge about your company and your industry sector may be quite shallow. So you have the opportunity to educate them a little in advance of the interview.

Knowledge – Information plus value equals knowledge. There is more than enough information flowing around any business – the ability to "cut" that information with business and communication objectives in mind is a real skill. Without knowledge, corporate reputation efforts amount to little more than pushing out a mass of information and hoping some of it sticks (or connects).

Local – Global businesses must never forget that their key audiences are all local at heart. Messages must be tailored or sensitized to their local needs with local examples of the company's policies and principles used in order make its communication stance relevant.

Without some effort at localization, the reputation of a business risks appearing distant and out of touch. Localization means connecting with the passions, values, and frame of reference of a local target market. All of this has to be achieved while maintaining global relevance. Masters at achieving this fine balance include Unilever (meeting the everyday needs of people everywhere) and McDonald's (''Glocalization'').

Management – Without good management there will not be good communication. Traditionally, companies have viewed PR as a way in which corporate deficiencies can be masked. No longer – you cannot communicate your way out of reality. The starting point in comprehensive and well-implemented reputation management comes down to the people running the company and what values that implicitly or explicitly represents. Within communication/PR agencies management is usually woeful.

News – News is a product – which means that it gets developed, manufactured, packaged, and distributed in the same way as any other type of fast-moving consumer good. It is vital for you to realize that news is produced within a commercial or business frame of reference and is therefore subject to the same operating principles.

The development of the story is similar to the R&D of a product; the writing of the story, or the TV production, is just an example of a manufacturing process; it is packaged with the consumer (that is, reader, listener, or viewer) in mind. And it gets distributed through cable, satellite, or newsstands in a very slick and sophisticated fashion. Let us not be under any illusion that news is a very fast-moving consumer good. Take Reuters Business Wire – it calibrates its success in getting a story to the market in tenths of a second.

Objective (business) – Communication activity must deliver against the business objective. Otherwise it will lack rigor.

Parker – Alan Parker (founder of Brunswick, the UK-based financial and corporate PR house – one of the most well-regarded privately owned PR businesses in the world) now boasts former White House spokesperson James Rubin as a partner.

Perception management – A concept which supports the methodologies and the organization of New York headquartered PR powerhouse Burson-Marsteller.

Quality – The move towards quality marques (such as ISO 9001) reached its climax in Europe in the late 1990s. Essentially, a series of processes and procedures were set out and implemented within PR agencies. Attaining and maintaining these ratifications proved arduous. The systems were also seen as overly bureaucratic and stifling of creativity. On the plus side, they helped the agencies to be consistent, as the hallmark of well-implemented quality systems is that you do what you say and you say what you do.

Royal Dutch/Shell – A year after the conflict over the dumping at sea of the oil platform the *Brent Spar*, Shell declared that the *"Brent Spar* is no longer just a North Sea installation, but a unique and defining event."* The pressure group Greenpeace, armed with inaccurate and incomplete science, successfully brought one of the world's most profitable companies to its knees. Later, Greenpeace actually apologized in a letter for getting it wrong – but this did not get in the way of a memorable victory. From the Shell perspective, the event proved to be a classic in misjudging public and governmental expectations; the incident cost the business heavily both in direct costs and in damage to its long-term corporate standing.

Sell more beer – A phrased used by August Busch III, head of Anheuser-Busch, the world's largest brewer. Interestingly, this command related to the company's commitment to protecting natural habitats, aluminum recycling, and other activities, voiced elsewhere in the report. Busch was creating the virtuous circle of enlightened self-interest. Help others but never forget that if we do not drive our business (which is selling beer) we won't be around to help anyone. It raises an important issue: how do the activities of a company and the ways in which they are presented influence sales activity?

Tylenol – The 1980s introduced a new era of public relations and corporate social responsibility. A seminal moment occurred when healthcare giant Johnson & Johnson was faced with one of the seminal moments in its corporate history, with its classic handling of the tylenol poisonings in 1983. This was an event which was to transform the need to manage one's reputation at a corporate level from being the occasional luxury of Fortune 500 players to being a necessity. For the first time, the world could see that open and frank dealings between a company and its stakeholders in times of extreme difficulty could ultimately be good for business. It was also visible that a core company belief (in this case the Credo) allowed consistent and credible messages to be disseminated.

Understanding – If a corporation can empathize with an outside body – be it an aggrieved member of the public or an antagonistic NGO – that company is in a much better position to communicate to and around them. Understanding an audience is not the same as agreeing with them. But the company which understands and listens is already at an advantage and has a greater chance of achieving its business objective within that scenario. Effective communication breaks down and one's reputation suffers when the company displays little or no empathy with the other party.

Validate – A term used in media training. The spokesperson becomes like an advocate for his or her own company. In this way they set out their stance and validate this stance using local and relevant examples of their messages in action. This is a particularly effective way of empowering the spokesperson and getting them out of the (usually) defensive mindset with which they approach the media. See: www.thebcf.com

WPP – The largest marketing group in the world – owner of Burson-Marsteller and Hill & Knowlton. Sir Martin Sorrell is its CEO.

Y&R – The global advertising agency which recently spawned new research claiming that brands are the new point of meaning in our lives – replacing religion.

Zen (less is more) – Effective communication is about selecting the right material for the right audience – rather than trying to spray a lot of information and hoping for the best.

Resources

Much has been written on the subject of reputation management. This chapter gives descriptions of some useful sources of information, including:

» books;
» seminal articles;
» organizations and associations;
» trade publications; and
» additional Websites.

RECOMMENDED BOOKS

Argenti, Paul A. (1997) *Corporate Communication*. McGraw-Hill Higher Education, New York.

Described as the most comprehensive corporate communications text on the market, including both text and cases.

Cannon, Tom (1994) *Corporate Responsibility: A Textbook on Business Ethics, Governance, Environment: Roles and Responsibilities*. Pitman Publishing, London.

A well-illustrated academic textbook, including case studies. Suitable for business students.

Caywood, Clarke L. (ed.) (1997) *The Handbook of Strategic Public Relations and Integrated Communications*. McGraw-Hill, New York.

Forty-five authors explore the field of public relations integrated communications as a professional area of study and practice. A rich source of knowledge and examples.

Cutlip, Scott M., Center, Allen H. & Broom, Glen M. (1999) *Effective Public Relations* (8th edn). Prentice Hall, Englewood Cliffs, NJ.

Described as the "bible" of public relations and one of the most authoritative and inclusive texts. Offers a worthwhile read on the history, theory, and practice of public relations.

Cutlip, Scott M. (1994) *The Unseen Power: Public Relations. A History*. Lawrence Erlbaum, Hillsdale, NJ.

Cutlip is a respected public relations scholar for whom this book represents the culmination of 40 years of research, making it largely an academic read. Provides an insight into PR history.

Fombrun, C. (1996) *Reputation: Realizing Value from the Corporate Image*. Harvard Business School Press, Cambridge, MA.

Management professor and executive director of the Reputation Institute, Charles Fombrun inquires into the workings of corporate reputation by looking at respected US companies and specific industries such as financial services and MBA schools. One of the most popularized books on reputation management.

Gladwell, Malcolm (2000) *The Tipping Point: How Little Things Can Make a Big Difference*. Little Brown, New York.

Highly readable and engaging book which looks at how epidemics are created, from the outbreak of TB to the success of hush puppies.

Goffee, Rob & Jones, Gareth *The Character of a Corporation: How Your Company's Culture Can Make or Break Your Business*. HarperCollins Business, New York.

An informative and thoughtful book which shows you how to characterize your own company.

Gregory, James R. & Wiechmann, Jack G. (contributor) (1997) *Leveraging the Corporate Brand*. NTC Business Books, Chicago.

Attempting to measure and value the impact of intangible assets on a company's bottom line. The discussion is complemented with practical ideas.

Hammer, Michael & Champy, James (1993) *Re-engineering the Corporation: A Manifesto for Business Revolution*. HarperCollins, New York.

An international best-seller and influential business book on drastically changing a company's processes, organization, and culture to significantly enhance performance. Described as the book that drove the re-engineering craze in all types of corporations on the 1990s.

Jolly, Adam (ed.) (2001) *Managing Corporate Reputations*. Kogan Page in association with Public Relations Consultants Association (PRCA), London.

The most recent book on reputation management concentrates on the importance of a company's reputation and the key role of the CEO in managing this intangible asset effectively. The 21 experts that contributed to the book agree that mishandling a corporation's reputation is a most significant threat to the career of the CEO.

Ind, Nicholas (1997) *The Corporate Brand*. New York University Press, New York.

The Corporate Brand sheds light onto how corporations create and manage their brands, reputation, and corporate identity.

Morley, Michael (1998) *How To Manage Your Global Reputation: A Guide to the Dynamics of International Public Relations*. New York University Press, New York.

Long-time international practitioner Michael Morley offers a probing study on public relations and its influence on corporate reputation.

Olasky, Marvin N. (1987) *Corporate Public Relations: A New Historical Perspective*. Lawrence Erlbaum, Hillsdale, NJ.

Offers an interesting angle from which to view the historical role of public relations, seen here as an attempt by corporations to limit competition.

Peters, Glen (1999) *Waltzing with the Raptors: A Practical Roadmap to Protecting Your Company's Reputation*. John Wiley & Sons, New York.

Easy-to-read and well-structured implementation guide to reputation assurance. It offers numerous examples and a sample reputation report. Overall the book succeeds in drawing attention to the importance of assets other than just the bottom line.

Riahi-Belkaoui, Ahmed & Pavlik, Ellen L. (1992) *Accounting for Corporate Reputation*. Greenwood Publishing Group, Westport, CT.

Focusing on US firms, the authors provide insights on corporate reputation, emphasizing the concepts of corporate social performance and organizational effectiveness. Recommended reading for firms and investors alike.

Riahi-Belkaoui, Ahmed (2000) *The Role of Corporate Reputation for Multinational Firms: Accounting, Organizational, and Market*

Considerations. Quorum Books, Greenwood Publishing Group, Westport, CT.

A comprehensive and insightful book on the most important factors determining corporate reputation. A suitable read for practitioners, academics, and investors.

Schultz, Majken (ed) (2000) *The Expressive Organization: Linking Identity, Reputation, and the Corporate Brand*. Oxford University Press, Oxford.

A largely academic review of issues relating to identity, reputation, branding, and communication.

Van Riel, C.B.M. & Blackburn, Chris (1995) *Principles of Corporate Communication*. Prentice Hall, Englewood Cliffs, NJ.

A cross-practice approach, integrating theory from the public relations tradition, and marketing communication.

SEMINAL ARTICLES

These are listed in date order, most recent first. A short extract of each follows.

Fombrun, Charles J. (2001) "The financial services reputation quotient – reputations – measurable, valuable, and manageable." *American Banker*, May 25.

"In 1998 I invited the market research firm of Harris Interactive to collaborate with the Reputation Institute in creating a standardized instrument that could be used to measure perceptions of companies across industries and with multiple stakeholder segments. We created and trademarked an index that sums up people's perceptions of companies on 20 attributes and called it the 'Reputation Quotient.'"

France, Stephanie (2001) "Reputation management – an ethical stake – socially responsible policies are now setting business agendas." *PR Week* (UK Version), April 20.

"There is little doubt that social responsibility is set to become part of the corporate landscape. And as the custodians of reputation, PR practitioners are uniquely placed to demonstrate how an ethical balance sheet can add value."

Griffin, Gerry (2000) "Survey – mastering management: how to say the right thing in the right way." *Financial Times*, December 18.

"Every comment from major companies is likely to be picked over by journalists and analysts. Gerry Griffin provides a step-by-step guide to communications strategy."

"Corporate communications is a way in which the corporate essence is expressed and consolidated. Used well, it can encourage transparency and build confidence that the business is doing what it says and saying what it does."

Fombrun, Charles J. (2000) "Survey – mastering management: the value to be found in corporate reputation." *Financial Times*, December 4.

"The public's view of a company not only acts as a reservoir of goodwill, but also boosts the bottom line. Charles Fombrun examines how perceptions can be measured.

"Reputation attracts resources to companies and enables them to operate. The essence of building reputations does not lie in posturing, spin-doctoring or puffery. Rather, it presents reputation management as a source of competitive advantage – which makes it nothing less than enlightened self-interest."

Prema, Nakra (2000) "Corporate Reputation Management – 'CRM' with a strategic twist?" *Public Relations Quarterly*, July 1.

"Corporate Reputation Management (CRM). Often contained within a corporate communications function, reputation management is about building a sound corporate reputation and maintaining the strength. A number of trends are converging to put enormous pressure on the modern corporation, and its relationship with the world. Several factors for the renewed interest in CRM are discussed.

"Global success in the twenty-first century will demand greater attention to building a favorable corporate image and leveraging the company's reputation by measuring and leveraging the intangible assets and knowledge resources, including but not limited to the corporate employees, customers and other stakeholders.''

Schmitt, Bernd (2000) ''Survey – mastering risk – branding puts a high value on reputation management.'' *Financial Times*, June 13.

''The author suggests best practice in reputation management requires considerable reflection and honesty. Virtually anything an enterprise does or says will either enhance or destroy brand value. Reputation management has become a natural extension of brand care – good reputations sell goods and services, poorly managed ones destroy shareholder value.''

Smy, Lucy (2000) ''Survey – standard bearers of best practice – corporate reputation.'' *Financial Times*, June 2.

''A variety of interests is now shaping companies' approach to everything from investment practice to social responsibility.

''These are the push factors – protesters and investors joining forces to ensure a level of acceptable behavior. But apart from the threat of censure, what are the attractions of social or environmental responsibility? Judging by the fact that more than three-quarters of the FTSE 200 companies are now members of Business in the Community, the charity that led the expansion of business social responsibility in the UK, the attractions must be quite strong.''

Anon. (2000) ''Measuring corporate reputation puts PR on management's A-list.'' *PR News*, **56**(22), May 29.

''Corporate reputation management has become a buzz phrase for the PR industry, spawning a whole new category of measurement. According to a Hill & Knowlton/Chief Executive Magazine survey, 96% of CEOs believe their company's reputation is important to business success. But only 19% have begun measuring reputation. Despite all the talk, a standard reputation yardstick is elusive.''

France, Stephanie (2000) ''Corporate reputation. Putting a caring face first.'' *PR Week* (UK Version), April 21.

"There's a difference between really getting involved, and just paying lip service to a good cause, which won't impress consumers. Whatever organizations a business chooses to associate itself with must be deep-rooted within its values."

Waddock, Sandra & Smith, Neil (2000) "Corporate responsibility audits – doing well by doing good." *Sloan Management Review (USA)*, January 1 .

"Responsibility audits are a management tool for demonstrating the potential qualitative and financial benefits of mirroring core values and ethics in practice. They direct managers' attention to socially responsible practices that meet the expectations of primary stakeholders. Achieving the benefits rests on creating an adaptive and proactive corporate culture from the top down. Such proactive management helps avoid normally hidden costs and liabilities that come from reacting to problems as they occur. Moreover, operating responsibly is – or can be – a core business strategy, one in which core operating functions are considered strategic, and stakeholder relationships and financial performance are allowed to grow."

Peters, Glen (1999) "Survey – world's most respected companies – why nice guys finish first – reputation management." *Financial Times*, December 7.

"The management of corporate reputation will become more complex. However, the companies that develop this new competence (outlined and explained in the article) – those we call 'the good guys' – will secure a more sustainable future not only for investors but also for employees, customers, and the societies in which they trade."

Boyle, Matthew (1999) "Corporate reputation – are we close to 'Holy Grail' of reputation?" *PR Week* (US Version), November 15.

"Reputation measurement tools are now a dime a dozen, but which one will the PR industry rally behind? With rival firms all pushing their own systems, can a consensus be reached? Matthew Boyle examines a leading contender, Reputation Quotient (RQ).

"Corporate reputation is difficult to evaluate without asking consumers (RQ). . . .'Anything that broadens [the Fortune list] and provides a bigger picture will help,' says Kirk Stewart, VP of communications at Nike. . . .The Council of Public Relations Firms, who released two studies earlier this year that made a strong case for increased investment in reputation management, has a dilemma on its hands: it wants to get behind a universal reputation measurement system, but it also supports the idea of multiple research vendors. In the end, it seems that creating new reputation tools is the easy part."

Capelin, Joan (President of Capelin Communications) (1999) "Search for reputation management standard is a noble one, but keep figures in perspective." *PR Week* (US Version), November 15.

"I applaud the 'hot ticket' status of reputation measurement that has engulfed PR Week's pages. . . .But while there is clearly a place for a consistent system to evaluate corporate status, it is not the Holy Grail of reputation management. Instead, such quantification is a tool, to be kept in healthy perspective by the reputation managers who drive the systems. . . .How to envision and choose options is not measurable, but they will remain the key to managing reputation – even if a measurement system is developed."

Boyle, Matthew (1999) "Reputation management." *PR Week* (US Version), June 28.

"New cash-reputation results impact clients. A strong connection has been established between PR spending and corporate reputation. Matthew Boyle gets the story behind the numbers.

"The study, conducted by Impulse Research (Los Angeles), provides the most compelling evidence to date of the irrefutable link between PR spending and corporate reputation. The Council found that companies in the top 200 in the Fortune survey spend more than twice as much on PR ($6mn) than companies with weaker reputations, who shell out only $2.8mn on average."

Hutton, James G. (1999) "The definition, dimensions, and domain of public relations." *Public Relations Review*, June 22.

"'The public relations occupation was too profitable for its benefi-ciaries to accept the reformation and reconstruction that paradigm changes require . . . The trade was made: acceptance of a low status for public relations in return for acceptance of fat paychecks.' While Olasky's assessment may or may not be accurate, his basic observation about the lack of theory development in public rela-tions appears to be correct. One of the primary purposes of the definition and framework presented here is to encourage the recog-nition and development of strategic relationships as the dominant paradigm that the public relations field so desperately needs if it hopes to advance in either theory or practice. While not without flaw, 'managing strategic relationships' offers a parsimonious defi-nition of public relations that is easily communicated, relevant for both theory and practice, and not so broad as to be meaningless nor so narrow as to be overly limiting."

Boyle, Matthew (1999) "Reputation management." *PR Week* (US Version), March 29.

"Disciples preach the gospel of PR's power/CEOs and marketing executives have been steadily promoting the viability of PR. Matthew Boyle investigates this remarkable sea change.

"There are [many] CEOs who have yet to discover the true power of PR. Among the non-believers, it's unlikely that most have an intractable distrust of PR; rather, they just haven't met one of the disciples yet. The arguments against using strategic communications – most notably, the difficulty in tracking return on investment – stand in the face of reams of research and a chorus of voices singing PR's praises."

Petrick, J.A., Scherer, R.F., Brodzinski, J.D., Quinn, J.F. & Ainina, M.F. (1999) "Global leadership skills and reputational capital: intan-gible resources for sustainable competitive advantage." *Academy of Management Executive*, **13**(1), 58–69.

"Two lessons at the firm – and industry – level on the impact of inadequate global leadership and wasted reputational capital are examined. Four management practices for improving strategic competitiveness are provided: global leadership skills, executive oversight responsibilities for global corporate reputation, an annual global reputation audit, and global awards and rankings to focus momentum on the key intangible resources for sustainable competitive advantage in the 21st century."

Joachimsthaler, E. & Aaker, D.A. (1997) "Building brands without mass media." *Harvard Business Review* (Section: World View), **75**(1), 189–96.

"Several companies in Europe have come up with alternative brand-building approaches and are blazing a trail in the post-media age. The various campaigns share characteristics that could serve as guidelines for any company hoping to build a successful brand: 1. Senior managers were carefully involved with brand-building efforts. 2. The companies recognized the importance of clarifying their core brand identity. 3. They made sure that all their efforts to gain visibility were tied to the core identity. Studying the methods of companies outside one's own industry and country can be instructive for managers."

Landry, J.T. (1997) "Corporate identity: seek substance over style." *Harvard Business Review* (Section: Briefings from the Editors), **75**(3), 12–13.

"Too many managers have overly optimistic expectations of what changes in names and logos can accomplish. The best that these symbols can do is to remind people of qualities that they already perceive in a company."

Pearson, Ron (1990) "Perspectives on public relations history." *Public Relations Review*, **16**(3).

A to-the-point account of historical public relations for the lay person.

ORGANIZATIONS AND ASSOCIATIONS

Council of Public Relations Firms

Website: www.prfirms.org

Membership: 122 firms, including all top 10 and 65% of the top 50 firms. Offerings: business programs, research, PR methodologies, guide to hiring a PR agency, talent programs, management programs, rankings, M&A reports, benchmarking surveys, business consulting services.

Institute for Public Relations (IPR)

Website: www.instituteforpr.com

First established by a group of senior public relations practitioners as the Foundation for Public Relations Research and Education, the IPR offers publications, lectures, awards, symposia, professional development forums, and other programs. IPR has also supported more than 200 separate research projects, practice-oriented programs and publications, awards, and competitions.

International Association of Business Communicators (IABC)

Website: www.iabc.com

As a 13,700-member not-for-profit worldwide association, IABC is a learning community for professionals committed to improving the effectiveness of organizations through strategic communication. IABC members practice the disciplines of corporate communication, employee/internal communication, marketing communication, public relations/external communication, media relations, community relations, public affairs, investor relations, and government relations.

International Communications Consultancy Organization (ICCO)

Website: www.martex.co.uk/prca/ico/index.htm

ICCO represents over 850 consultancies, employing over 25,000 people in 24 nations around the globe.

Through regular surveys of members and extensive research, ICCO represents the views and opinions of ICCO members, and ensures their voice is heard.

International Public Relations Association (IPRA)

Website: www.ipranet.org

IPRA constitutes an international grouping of public relations practitioners, active in promoting exchange of information and co-operation in every sector of the profession, as well as in building a program of professional development opportunities and other initiatives aimed at enhancing the role of public relations in management and international affairs. IPRA has members in 82 countries.

National Investor Relations Institute (NIRI)

Website: www.niri.org

NIRI is a professional association of corporate officers and investor relations consultants responsible for communication among corporate management, the investing public, and the financial community. It has over 5,000 members in 31 chapters around the US. Among others NIRI offers seminars, text and trade books, reprints of articles, audio tapes, and survey reports.

Public Relations Consultants Association (PRCA)

Website: www.martex.co.uk/prca/index.htm

The trade association represents 70% of the UK's public relations consultancies. Its members are 128 consultancy brands of all sizes. The PRCA provides a forum for government and other public bodies and associations to talk to public relations consultants, and represents the views of its members to the DTI, other bodies, and the media.

Public Relations Society of America (PRSA)

Website: www.prsa.org

PRSA is the world's largest organization for public relations professionals. It has nearly 20,000 members, organized worldwide in over 100 chapters. The Society provides professional development opportunities through continuing education programs, information exchange forums, and research projects conducted on the national and local levels.

The Counselors' Academy

Website: www.prsa-counselors.org

The Academy, PRSA's oldest and largest professional interest section, has been, for over 40 years, a business resource for professional public relations counselors worldwide. Academy members range from solo practitioners to senior executives who manage multinational public relations firms. Members are accredited members of the Public Relations

Society of America or the Canadian Public Relations Society, or meet an equivalency standard that includes ten years in the public relations field.

TRADE PUBLICATIONS

Corporate Reputation Review

Editors: Charles Fombrun, New York University; Cees B. M. van Riel, Erasmus University, The Netherlands. Henry Stewart Publications.

International quarterly journal published by the Reputation Institute that provides in-depth, cutting edge articles, case studies, and conceptual papers on recent developments, latest thinking, and best practice in reputation management.

PR Week (US)

Website: www.prweek.com

First weekly magazine to offer nationwide coverage of public relations business. Latest industry news, in-depth analysis. and reviews of campaigns.

PR Week (UK)

Website: www.prweek.com

Editor: Kate Nicholas.

UK edition of *PR Week*. An essential read for PR professionals. Published weekly.

Corporate Communications: An International Journal

Website: www.emeraldinsight.com/ccij.htm

A *Corporate Communications* subscription includes four printed issues per year plus online access to the current and previous volumes via Emerald Fulltext. It addresses the theory and practice arising from corporate communications which lie at the heart of effective strategic management, planning, and control.

Journal of Communication Management

Website: www.henrystewart.com/journals/jcm

Published in association with the Institute of Public Relations and the International Association of Business Communicators (Europe and

Africa). Both on paper and online, the journal provides in-depth, peer-reviewed, practitioner-oriented articles from leading consultants and agents, blue chips, and academics at the forefront of practice and theory of stakeholder communication.

O'Dwyer Newsletter

Website: www.odwyerpr.com/jack_odwyers_nl/current.htm

A weekly eight-page newsletter with information for the PR professional.

Public Relations Review

Website: www.elsevier.com/locate/pubrev

The *Public Relations Review* contains major articles, notes on research in brief, book reviews, and précis of new books. It is published five times a year and is also available online.

Public Relations Quarterly

Editor: Howard Penn Hudson.

United States publication covering all aspects of public relations.

ADDITIONAL WEBSITES

The Reputation Institute

www.reputationinstitute.com

Private research organization founded by Prof. Charles Fombrun, Stern School of Business, New York University and Prof. Cees van Riel, Rotterdam School of Management, Erasmus University. The Institute's mission is to build thought leadership about corporate reputations, their management, measurement, and valuation. It brings together a global network of academic institutions and leading edge practitioners interested in advancing knowledge on corporate reputations. Provides information on research, publications, conferences, and resources.

Reputation Management

www.reputations.org

This site is developed and hosted by the Reputation Institute with funding provided by Shandwick International and Federal Express. Information about corporate reputation, resources, the journal *Corporate Reputation Review*, rankings, and research.

CEOgo.com
www.ceogo.com

Website launched by Burson-Marsteller, the global communications consulting firm. Provides information on how to position a company and maximize its reputation in the eyes of key stakeholders and the public as a whole. See also www.bm.com/insights/corpresp.html which links to Burson-Marsteller's Corporate Social Responsibility Unit, a team whose members have experience of the public sector as well as working with NGOs.

PR Newswire
www.prnewswire.com

PR Newswire offers communications services for public relations and investor relations professionals, ranging from information distribution and market intelligence to the creation of online multimedia content and investor relations Websites.

PR & Marketing Network
www.prandmarketing.com

PRMN is a resource for expert news and strategies on PR and marketing. Free service from the publishers of *PR News*.

O'Dwyer's PR Daily Website
www.odwyerpr.com

O'Dwyer's PR Daily Website posts news and features throughout the day. The Website contains a database of more than 400 PR firms, a searchable client database, a database of PR service firms in 58 categories, job listings, O'Dwyer's newsletter, the latest PR books, articles on PR, upcoming PR events, and other features.

Online Public Relations Directory
www.online-pr.com

PR resources, media, and references.

Directory of Public Relations Agencies and Resources
www.impulse-research.com/prlist.html

Ten Steps to Making Reputation Management Work

1 Review business objective
2 Assess corporate culture
3 Review business actions
4 Set communication objectives
5 Assess current communication activities
6 Assess the mindset and behavior of key audiences involved
7 Develop key messages
8 Select the best delivery options
9 Align messages with delivery options
10 Develop a tactical plan.

In this final chapter, we put the pieces back together again. I would like to use a concrete example to show each of the ten steps applied to a specific situation. The example I would like to use is that of a brewery, situated in the middle of a residential area. The communications challenges it needs to overcome will fill out the structure of the key steps.

1. REVIEW BUSINESS OBJECTIVE

This provides the cornerstone of your activity and the benchmark of your success. Your business reputation should not be an ad hoc, last-minute activity – but thought through from the very beginning.

BREWERY BUSINESS OBJECTIVE
Increase capacity at facility by 50%.

2. ASSESS CORPORATE CULTURE

Corporate culture is expressed as the way in which the specific facility operates. How has it interacted with its surrounding community? What are industrial relations like? What is the dominant culture (in terms of sociability and solidarity)? See Chapter 2.

BREWERY CORPORATE CULTURE
Networked organization – high sociability and low solidarity. This means that informal networks are very important for the business. It also indicates that informal channels might be a key way in which the brewery could communicate most effectively with the local community.

3. REVIEW BUSINESS ACTIONS

You cannot communicate your way out of reality – so it is vital that the communications activity complements the business actions which arise out of the business objectives. Expansion requires a host of business actions.

BREWERY BUSINESS ACTIONS

Considerations include:

» investment decisions;
» planning applications (the facility needs to be expanded onto a field used by local residents, though the land is owned by the business);
» tendering processes;
» project management teams;
» construction;
» disruption of working patterns;
» increased noise and dust;
» increased employment; and
» modification of timetable in which stock is collected and materials delivered (because of greater volume).

4. SET COMMUNICATION OBJECTIVES

This will involve identifying where communications can have a significant impact. As a rule of thumb, decide what types of audience will have a meaningful impact on the business objective being realized. Affecting the perceptions or the behaviors of these audiences will be vital.

BREWERY COMMUNICATION OBJECTIVES

In the fictional plant, collecting stock and delivering is based on an 18-hour rotation: 6am to 12pm. The facility is in the middle of a residential area. The new distribution timetable is for 24-hour delivery and collection, with lorries filled with empty bottles rattling over speed ramps, past sleeping residents. This needs careful handling. Communication objectives would include expediting planning approval and minimizing negative reaction from community groups at the stages of planning application, construction, and operation.

5. ASSESS CURRENT COMMUNICATION ACTIVITIES

What is the business doing locally? The business always has a reputation – the question is: what are you doing to manage it? Start with an assessment of current activity, formal and informal, in order to be able to set realistic communications objectives. For example, it would be unrealistic to try to recruit to your agenda an audience (e.g. an NGO) which has always been antagonistic.

BREWERY CURRENT COMMUNICATION ACTIVITIES

Current activities might include sponsoring a local football team, funding conservation, and so on. The fewer "wheels" that need reinventing, the better.

6. ASSESS THE MINDSET AND BEHAVIOR OF KEY AUDIENCES INVOLVED

See Chapter 2 for the full set of audiences.

BREWERY MINDSET ASSESSMENT

The brewery should start with the local community, planning officials, employees who live locally, employees generally, media, and the financial community. It needs to be realistic – some independent research may be needed to set its bearings properly. The assessment should start with where each audience is now – rather than where the company would like them to be. It is important to be careful to determine which are attitudes that are likely to determine their behavior and which are just "passive" attitudes. It is the former has to be planned around. Required mindset/behavior change should be determined. Any strong negative views of the company need to be improved or marginalized. If 24-hour distribution is not negotiable, for example, what could be done to keep the affected audience on board? Where there are positive views, they should be marshaled in the company's defense, such as the value as a local employer and taxpayer.

7. DEVELOP KEY MESSAGES

These are the essence of your stance. They are also designed to move an audience (as in step 6).

BREWERY'S KEY MESSAGES

In the case of the local stance on taxation (probably aimed at planning officials) the message might be: "Without expansion, the plant will not be competitive, so endangering jobs (and taxes)."

8. SELECT THE BEST DELIVERY OPTIONS

When you need to identify, recruit, educate, and mobilize third parties to speak on your behalf, do you contact people directly in open meetings, or by letter, or generically, through the media?

BREWERY CHANNELS

These include:

» an open day inviting the media and the local community to see the facility - the new plans - and to find out the rationale behind the expansion;
» an informal meeting with local community leaders;
» detailed briefings with planning officials; and
» proactive media relations.

9. ALIGN MESSAGES WITH DELIVERY OPTIONS

Make sure the right people are set up to give the right messages. Local managers are often best for dealing with local issues. Press officers need to be trained. Third parties need to be given information and support materials.

10. DEVELOP A TACTICAL PLAN

Timing is particularly important here – making sure you get the right messages to the right audiences through the right channels. For example, there is little point delivering the right message to the planning officials too late for it to have an effect.

CONCLUSION

Corporate communications is a way in which the corporate essence is expressed and consolidated. Used well, it can encourage transparency and build confidence that the business is doing what it says and saying what it does.

Frequently Asked Questions (FAQs)

Q1: Why should managing my reputation make any difference to our business?

A: Good reputation management can help the achievement of the business objective. It can increase transparency and help build confidence inside and outside the business. See Chapter 1 and Chapter 10.

Q2: What you mean by communication?

A: Your need to differentiate between information and communication. Communication impacts on behavior. See Chapter 1 and Chapter 10.

Q3: How long has the formal practice of reputation management been around?

A: Since the beginning of the 20th century, but the notion of the "corporate brand" is very recent. See Chapter 6.

Q4: Whose opinions do we need to care about most?

A: The full range of audiences are detailed in Chapter 2.

Q5: What happens if we just ignore our reputation?

A: If ignored, the company can experience a series of issues or crises which impact on sales: see Coca-Cola in Chapter 2 and Nike in Chapter 5.

Q6: Do the rules of the game change within the digital economy?

A: Very much so – the need for global consistency is greatly increased. The pressure on corporate transparency and speed of response on key issues is also increased. See Chapter 4.

Q7: What does the much-talked-about subject of corporate social responsibility really mean?

A: Loosely, how a corporate's reputation plays out in environmental terms. See Chapter 6.

Q8: Does the practice of reputation management change around the world?

A: The principles are largely the same, the tactical plans may change depending on indigenous conditions. See Chapter 7, the section "Unilever in China".

Q9: Does corporate reputation largely revolve around the corporate mission statement?

A: Actually words are the least of the issue – it is to do with deeds, behavior, and values. Words may sum up the policy but a business, mindful of its reputation, will match deeds with policy. See Chapter 6, where there is some backlash to worthy words but fewer deeds in the area of CSR.

Q10: Where can I find out more about the subject?

A: Much has been said on the subject and you can find a detailed set of resources in Chapter 9.

Acknowledgments

Many thanks to Stuart and Des – gurus of Suntop Media. I would also like to thank Nick Bent and Emmanuella Tsapouli of Burson-Marsteller. Also many thanks to Karl Griffin for the research input.

Chapters 2 and 10 make use of methodologies and material developed in training sessions co-hosted by Paul Gillions.

I cannot leave out a special source of inspiration, which is the Finsbury Centre squad of Aidan, Goody, Grant, Sacha, Austyn, Donal, Mike, Doug, Chas, and Neville. Finally, I would also like to mention the one and only Chas Cleaver.

Index